Intermediate

100%® Listening

Skill Area:	Listening Skills
Ages:	8 through 10
Grades:	3 through 5

LinguiSystems

LinguiSystems, Inc.
3100 4th Avenue
East Moline, IL 61244
800-776-4332
FAX: 800-577-4555
E-mail: service@linguisystems.com
Web: linguisystems.com

Printed in the U.S.A.

ISBN 10: 0-7606-0394-4
ISBN 13: 978-0-7606-0394-9

Edited by Karen Stontz
Illustrated by Margaret Warner
Page Layout by Christine Buysse
Cover Design by Chris Claus

Table of Contents

Introduction 5

Repetition 7

Answering Questions 17

Following Directions 30

Categories 43

Riddles 56

Asking Questions for Comprehension 64

Paraphrasing 79

Identifying Details 94

Main Idea 106

Differentiating Speakers' Purposes 116

Grammar 122

Inferences 143

Extending Conversations 153

Nonverbal Communication 159

Introduction

Effective listening is the foundation for successful communication in school, at home, and in everyday situations. Students with undeveloped listening skills are at risk for academic and social difficulties. Most of these students have adequate hearing, yet they don't know what it means to "listen carefully." They have no strategies to think about what they hear in order to understand and remember the information. They need training and practice in being active listeners — thinking purposefully about what they hear in order to respond or take appropriate action.

Good listening requires more than just paying attention. Listeners need to take responsibility to seek clarification when they don't understand something. They need to hold what they hear in their memories well enough to reflect on the information. What associations can students make between new information and what they already know? What does or doesn't make sense about the information? Were there nonverbal messages that colored what someone actually said? What are they supposed to do about the information that was presented? Is all of the information equally important? How should they program themselves to remember any important information?

100% Listening — Intermediate will teach students in third through fifth grade to pay active attention to what they hear. Students practice active listening in structured interactions that mirror classroom and everyday situations. Each unit features a specific listening skill with enough stimuli to help students master the skill in a training or instructional context. The sequence of the skills reflects general language and thinking skill development, although skill areas overlap each other considerably. These skills are featured in this book:

- Repetition
- Answering Questions
- Following Directions
- Categories
- Riddles
- Asking Questions for Comprehension
- Paraphrasing
- Identifying Details
- Main Idea
- Differentiating Speakers' Purposes
- Grammar
- Inferences
- Extending Conversations
- Nonverbal Communication

We believe almost all students can improve their ability to attend to, process, and respond to what they hear. Improving students' listening skills will also improve their thinking and social skills. We hope the activities in *100% Listening — Intermediate* will help your students to use effective listening and thinking skills in the classroom and beyond.

Repetition

In this unit, paying attention is reinforced as students repeat or copy what they hear in a variety of listening tasks.

Clapping Patterns
On page 8, students copy the clapping patterns they hear. The difficulty of the patterns vary, ranging in length from three to six claps.

On page 9, students copy patterns that vary along the two parameters of loudness and timing. The items range in length from three to six claps.

Words
Words in this task are taken from curricular reading materials and other words familiar to students in grades 3 through 5. The items are arranged in difficulty, starting with short words/short lists and moving through items to longer words/longer lists. Lists range in length from three to five words in each task.

On page 10, students repeat lists of related words.
On page 11, students repeat lists of unrelated words.

Numbers
Numbers to repeat are presented in everyday, meaningful contexts (e.g., giving license numbers, locker combinations, zip codes, and phone numbers). The stimulus items begin with easy ones to remember and progress to more difficult items.

Proper Nouns
Words in this task are taken from curricular reading materials and other words familiar to students in grades 3 through 5. The items are arranged in difficulty, starting with lists of three related proper nouns and progressing to lists of five unrelated proper nouns.

On page 13, students repeat lists of related words.
On page 14, students repeat lists of unrelated words.

Sentences
Items range in difficulty from simple, short sentences to complex, longer sentences. They are presented in meaningful contexts of giving information and/or directions.

Chanting Games
Students repeat sentences that get longer and longer as you add items to the original list. You can present these items as a simple repetition task or make it a game by taking turns. To play the game, each person repeats the previous sentence and then adds an item to the list. See who can remember the longest sentence.

Repetition 1

Say, "Listen carefully. Clap like I do."

(Note: A bullet indicates a one-second pause in clapping.)

1. clap • clap, clap

2. clap • clap, clap • clap

3. clap, clap • clap

4. clap, clap, clap • clap

5. clap • clap, clap • clap

6. clap, clap • clap, clap

7. clap, clap, clap, clap • clap

8. clap • clap, clap, clap • clap

9. clap • clap • clap • clap, clap

10. clap • clap, clap • clap

11. clap • clap • clap, clap • clap

12. clap, clap • clap • clap, clap

13. clap, clap, clap • clap • clap

14. clap, clap • clap • clap

15. clap • clap • clap • clap, clap

16. clap • clap, clap, clap • clap

17. clap • clap • clap, clap, clap

18. clap, clap, clap, clap • clap

19. clap • clap, clap • clap • clap

20. clap, clap, clap • clap, clap

21. clap • clap, clap, clap, clap, clap

22. clap • clap, clap, clap • clap • clap

23. clap, clap • clap, clap, clap • clap

24. clap, clap, clap • clap, clap • clap

25. clap • clap • clap, clap • clap, clap

Repetition 2

Say, "Listen carefully. Clap like I do."

(Note: A bullet indicates a one-second pause in clapping. Capitals indicate a loud clap.)

1. clap • CLAP, clap

2. clap • clap, CLAP, CLAP

3. CLAP, CLAP • clap

4. clap, clap, CLAP • clap

5. CLAP, CLAP • clap, CLAP

6. CLAP • CLAP • CLAP, clap

7. CLAP, clap • clap, CLAP

8. clap • CLAP • clap, CLAP

9. CLAP • CLAP, clap

10. clap, CLAP, CLAP • clap

11. CLAP, clap, clap • CLAP

12. CLAP • CLAP • clap, CLAP

13. clap, clap • CLAP • clap

14. CLAP • clap, clap • CLAP

15. CLAP, clap, clap • CLAP

16. clap, clap • CLAP, CLAP

17. clap • CLAP • CLAP • clap

18. CLAP, clap, CLAP • CLAP

19. clap, CLAP, clap, CLAP • CLAP

20. clap, clap, CLAP, CLAP, clap • CLAP

21. CLAP • CLAP • clap, clap, CLAP • clap

22. clap • clap • CLAP • CLAP • clap, CLAP

23. clap • CLAP • clap, clap • CLAP, CLAP

24. clap, CLAP, CLAP, CLAP, clap • clap

25. CLAP • clap, clap, clap • CLAP, CLAP

Repetition 3

Say, "Listen carefully. Say these words after me."

1. city, county, state

2. square, rectangle, circle

3. telescope, planet, magnify

4. century, decade, era

5. fraction, decimal, percent

6. farmer, merchant, plantation, slavery

7. mass, volume, density, property

8. protest, vote, patriotic, justice

9. cone, sphere, cube, pyramid

10. sentence, paragraph, indent, topic

11. history, science, geometry, language arts

12. art, contrast, line, pattern, movement

13. letter, greeting, closing, address, body

14. rock, mineral, geology, microscope, crystal

15. classical, jazz, folk, ballet, tap dance

16. plateau, ocean, plains, wetlands, forest

17. birth, death, reproduction, growth, life cycle

18. nonfiction, biography, fiction, poetry, folk tale

19. appendix, table of contents, glossary, title, pages

20. abolitionist, colony, rebellion, confederate, constitution

Repetition 4

Say, "Listen carefully. Say these words after me."

1. safety, population, employment

2. prescription, harmony, politics

3. opponent, invasion, latitude

4. disability, resources, database

5. responsibility, basketball, technology

6. health, soccer, culture, taxpayer

7. rights, tools, trade, submarines

8. transportation, frontier, events, angle

9. protractor, diagram, encyclopedia, suspense

10. internet, continent, photograph, demonstration

11. point-of-view, adverb, measuring, parallel

12. weather, death, globe, modem, edit

13. program, routine, lifestyle, invention, mayor

14. disease, vocabulary, politics, character, vowel

15. consequence, leader, commerce, volume, fact

16. graph, summary, revolution, migrant, soprano

17. tornado, fossils, national, network, governor

18. diplomacy, military, floods, mining, soil

19. composition, reference, margin, warfare, court

20. dribble, apostrophe, agreement, imagery, peninsula

Repetition 5

Say, "We use numbers when we give license numbers. Say these license numbers after me."

1. 294 UBY

2. CFP 829

3. 392 JKW

4. 279 HJP

5. 918 WQE

6. 2 XYA 5

7. 925 FLZ

8. 479 AMH

9. EOL 783

10. B 386 GT

Say, "We use numbers when we give locker combinations. Say these combinations after me."

1. 3-6-9

2. 12-8-3

3. 14-26-2

4. 40-12-8

5. 14-2-93

6. 4-68-92

7. 83-29-51

8. 17-22-34

9. 25-90-73

10. 31-54-79

Say, "We use numbers when we give zip codes. Say these zip codes after me."

1. 52807

2. 63422

3. 09459

4. 74987

5. 29097

6. 63438

7. 12937

8. 49782

9. 23654-1404

10. 87077-2300

Say, "We use numbers to tell our phone numbers. Say these phone numbers after me."
(Note: First say the numbers individually. If the student has difficulty, then group the numbers to aid recall [e.g., three-two-two ninety-nine seventy].)

1. 322-9970

2. 338-8838

3. 234-7492

4. 876-2497

5. 243-8935

6. 563-9063

7. 482-9302

8. 259-2938

9. 302-8290

10. 935-8429

Repetition 6

Say, "Repeat these words after me."

1. Washington, Hancock, Jefferson

2. Greece, Kenya, Haiti

3. Vietnamese, Cuban, European

4. Daniel Boone, Sally Ride, Henry Ford

5. New Orleans, Sacramento, Seattle

6. Mayan, Portuguese, Roman

7. Statue of Liberty, Jefferson Memorial, Independence Hall

8. Israel, Korea, Cuba, Hungary

9. French, Italian, Spanish, German

10. Connecticut, New Jersey, Maryland, Virginia

11. Civil War, Vicksburg, Fort Sumter, Chattanooga

12. Thanksgiving, Labor Day, Presidents' Day, Memorial Day

13. Mercury, Pontiac, Nissan, Porsche, Chevrolet

14. Jacob, Keisha, Ethan, Adam, Carlos

15. Math, Science, Geography, Health, Spanish

16. Cartier, Magellan, Balboa, Columbus, Drake

17. Earth, Venus, Pluto, Saturn, Mars

18. Mississippi, Nile, Amazon, Hudson, Potomac

19. Hopi, Iroquois, Cherokee, Pueblo, Inca

20. Persia, Socrates, Sparta, Alexander, Cyrus

Repetition 7

Say, "Repeat these words after me."

1. Mohawk, Earhart, Pepsi

2. Ohio, Geronimo, Asia

3. Mazda, Earth, Leesa

4. Puerto Rico, Math, Cherokee

5. San Francisco, John Glenn, Braille

6. African-American, Eric the Red, English

7. Inuit, Burger King, Hanging Gardens

8. History, Italian, Dust Bowl, Peru

9. New York, Moslem, Ford, Nintendo

10. Mayflower, Roman, Ferdinand, Concord

11. New Orleans, Columbia, Shay, Beethoven

12. Bill of Rights, PlayStation, Jordan, Paris

13. Taj Mahal, Plymouth, Cortes, Saturday

14. Tubman, McDonald's, Wednesday, Mexican, Shiloh

15. Egyptian, Canada, Oneida, Adams, November

16. Black Hawk, Arctic, Timbuktu, Lexington, Atlantic

17. DuBois, Bering, Hancock, Pacific, Confederacy

18. Zane, Mozart, Tecumseh, Missouri, Monopoly

19. Babylon, Bantu, Philadelphia, Hamilton, Geometry

20. Armistead, Quebec, New England, Martin Luther King, Africa

Proper Nouns

100% Listening – Intermediate   14

Repetition 8

Say, "We use sentences to give information. Repeat these sentences after me."

1. The President of the United States heads the executive branch.

2. Pioneers on the plains could not cut wood to build houses.

3. Animals that hunt other animals for food are called predators.

4. About 80,000 people rushed to California to look for gold in 1849.

5. The Andes stretch the length of South America from north to south.

6. A place where living and nonliving things interact is called an ecosystem.

7. The first units of length used in Egypt were based on the body parts of a pharaoh.

8. The astronauts had fun hopping around like kangaroos in the moon's low gravity.

9. If you danced the flamenco for an hour, you would burn about 300 calories.

10. Friction is a force that makes it hard for two objects in contact to move past each other.

Say, "We use sentences to give directions. Repeat these sentences after me."

1. Write the action verb in each sentence.

2. Name three reasons why immigrants came to the United States.

3. Take the subway under Market Street to 6th Street.

4. Write the adjective or the adverb that correctly completes each sentence.

5. Measure to the nearest inch and then to the nearest half inch.

6. Pour the water into a measuring cup to find the capacity.

7. Write an article that tells about how people deal with the challenges of the climate in your state.

8. Make a chart to show how many more horseshoe crabs than jellyfish were found.

9. Diagram the linking verb and the two parts of the sentence that it joins.

10. Figure out how many combinations you can make if you mix three juices in equal amounts.

Repetition 9

Say, "Repeat these sentences after me."

1. My family is going camping. We need to bring a tent.

2. My family is going camping. We need to bring a tent and sleeping bags.

3. My family is going camping. We need to bring a tent, sleeping bags, and a change of clothes.

4. My family is going camping. We need to bring a tent, sleeping bags, a change of clothes, and flashlights.

5. My family is going camping. We need to bring a tent, sleeping bags, a change of clothes, flashlights, and some batteries.

6. My family is going camping. We need to bring a tent, sleeping bags, a change of clothes, flashlights, some batteries, and a radio.

7. My family is going camping. We need to bring a tent, sleeping bags, a change of clothes, flashlights, some batteries, a radio, and our toothbrushes.

8. My family is going camping. We need to bring a tent, sleeping bags, a change of clothes, flashlights, some batteries, a radio, our toothbrushes, and some toothpaste.

9. My family is going camping. We need to bring a tent, sleeping bags, a change of clothes, flashlights, some batteries, a radio, our toothbrushes, some toothpaste, and food to cook on the grill.

10. My family is going camping. We need to bring a tent, sleeping bags, a change of clothes, flashlights, some batteries, a radio, our toothbrushes, some toothpaste, food to cook on the grill, and lots of bottled water.

Make up your own chanting game. Take turns repeating what the previous person said and adding one more item. Here are some starting phrases.

I won a shopping spree at the mall. I'm going to buy . . .

Our class went on a field trip to a museum. We . . .

The astronauts blasted off in their space shuttle. They . . .

We're going to an amusement park. We're going to . . .

Answering Questions

Students answer an enormous amount of questions throughout the day. In fact, some researchers estimate that students spend at least 40% of the school day listening to and answering questions. Because of this, it's easy to see why these skills are so critical to students' success at school.

We give students a lot of information orally in the form of lectures, directions, explanations, announcements, etc. Often, we check their retention of this information by asking questions. Students who answer questions well:

- Pay attention or concentrate on the question.
- Understand the question and attach it to information they have in their brains.
- Know the vocabulary used in the question.
- Understand what type of answer the question requires.
- Have enough time to process the question, sort through their memories, review the vocabulary, and formulate their answers.

This unit gives students valuable practice answering a variety of question forms. In addition, the following is a list of practical tips for you to keep in mind to help your students answer questions more effectively.

- Make sure students are looking at you.
- Remove or reduce distractions in the room.
- Remove or reduce any emotional distractions students may have by helping them solve a problem or by reassuring them you'll get back to them later.
- Remove or reduce any physical issues that may make it hard for students to attend. Move a student closer to you or provide a snack as a mid-morning pick-me-up.
- Cue active listening by telling students to listen for a specific date, event, word, etc.
- Help students distinguish between tasks that require high levels of attention and those that do not. Let students relax during the low times.
- Make sure students have enough prior information about the subject area so they can connect the question to something they know. Find out what prior information they have and how accurate it is. Then fill in the gaps.
- Help students distinguish between important and unimportant information they hear.
- Explain why you are asking questions and why some details are important.
- Teach new vocabulary by incorporating definitions, synonyms, and antonyms, or by using words in analogies or songs.
- Review the question words *who, what, where, when, why,* and *how* and discuss what they mean.
- Teach other question forms and what type of responses they require.
- Give your students enough processing time before expecting an answer.
- During the "think" time, you might repeat the question to keep students focused on the task, to review vocabulary, or to re-read a passage.

Answering Questions 1

Say, "Listen to each question. Then answer *yes* or *no*. If your answer is *no*, give a reason for it."

1. If your TV remote isn't working, should you plug it in? *(no; TV remotes are powered by batteries, not electricity.)*

2. Would you wear a sweat suit on a hot summer day? *(no; sweat suit is too warm)*

3. Can you ride a bicycle if you have a broken leg? *(no; have a cast with a broken leg)*

4. Should a baby play with scissors? *(no; He might hurt himself.)*

5. If someone is frightened, is she afraid? *(yes)*

6. If your teacher is sick, do you get to stay home from school? *(no; teacher will stay home)*

7. If you wanted to eat fruit, would you eat green beans? *(no; Green beans are vegetables.)*

8. Can you take a train across the ocean? *(no; Train tracks don't go all the way across the ocean.)*

9. Could you look in an encyclopedia to find out more about beavers? *(yes)*

10. If you were playing hide-and-seek, would you be by yourself? *(no; play hide-and-seek with others)*

11. Does a dentist operate on people's hearts? *(no; dentist works on teeth)*

12. Can you change your birth date to a different date? *(no; can't change the day you were born)*

13. If you can't find your toothbrush, should you use someone else's? *(no; too many germs)*

14. Can you paint a picture of green grass if you only have blue and yellow paint? *(yes)*

15. If you need to study for your math test, should you write your spelling words? *(no; would study math problems)*

16. Can you run without moving your feet? *(no; Feet have to move to run.)*

17. If the doctor tells you to get plenty of rest and drink lots of fluids, should you play baseball? *(no; baseball isn't resting)*

18. Should you give someone your library book for a birthday present? *(no; Library books must be returned.)*

Answering Questions 2

Say, "Answer these questions."

1. What does the Sun look like? *(big, bright, yellow)*

2. Who helps people when they are sick? *(doctor, nurse, surgeon, parent)*

3. What does sandpaper feel like? *(rough, scratchy)*

4. What does snow feel like? *(cold, wet, hard, soft, fluffy)*

5. What is a thermometer used for? *(to take someone's temperature, to measure the temperature outside)*

6. Which holiday do you like better, Thanksgiving or Fourth of July? *(Answers will vary.)*

7. What do mail carriers do with letters? *(deliver them to homes and businesses, take them to the post office)*

8. What do sanitation workers do with garbage? *(pick it up and put it in garbage trucks; take it to landfills)*

9. What do people put in cars to make them run? *(gas)*

10. Who is the leader of a country? *(president, king)*

11. Which one is used to type something, a book or a computer? *(computer)*

12. What ingredients are in a pizza? *(dough, sauce, meat, cheese, vegetables)*

13. What do you need to know to make a telephone call? *(phone number)*

14. Who flies an airplane? *(pilot)*

15. What happens when you don't do your homework? *(get in trouble, get a zero)*

16. Which color is not found in the American flag: red, blue, or purple? *(purple)*

17. Who takes your money in a store? *(cashier)*

18. What happens when the fire alarm goes off at school? *(Everyone goes outside.)*

19. What would happen if someone touched boiling water? *(get burned)*

21. What might happen if you forget to set your alarm? *(might get up late)*

22. Who is your mother's sister? *(aunt)*

23. Which would a child play with, a scooter or a chainsaw? *(scooter)*

24. What happens when you return overdue library books? *(have to pay a fine)*

Answering Questions 3

Say, "Answer these questions."

1. When do we have dessert? *(after a meal)*

2. Where can you get vegetables? *(grocery store, garden)*

3. Where can you find a sink? *(bathroom, kitchen, laundry room, classroom)*

4. When is Valentine's Day? *(February 14th)*

5. Where are your lungs? *(in your chest, in your body [Child may point to indicate answer.])*

6. When do you see a rainbow? *(after it rains if the sun is shining)*

7. When would someone call 911? *(when there's an emergency)*

8. Where does a woman go to have a baby? *(hospital)*

9. When should you return your library books? *(on or before the due date)*

10. Where are a Ferris wheel, cotton candy, noise, and tickets found? *(carnival, fair, amusement park)*

11. When do leaves fall off trees? *(fall/autumn)*

12. Where should we cross the street? *(at the corner, in the crosswalk)*

13. Where do people put their money to keep it safe? *(bank, piggy bank, safe, etc.)*

14. When do babies cry? *(when they're hungry, sad, tired, have a wet diaper, etc.)*

15. When do people use luggage? *(when they go on trips)*

16. When might you say "Excuse me" to someone? *(when you bump into the person, when you burp or pass gas, when you want the person to repeat something she just said)*

17. Where might you see a robin's egg? *(in a nest, in a tree, on the ground)*

18. When should you stay home from school? *(on the weekends, on a holiday, when you're sick, when school is cancelled)*

19. When do we go to a funeral? *(when someone we know dies)*

20. Where is the Statue of Liberty? *(New York City)*

21. Where do bats live? *(caves, trees, attics)*

22. Where does wool come from? *(sheep)*

Answering Questions 4

Say, "Answer these questions."

1. How many eggs are in a dozen? *(12)*

2. Why should you change your clothes after you get wet in the rain? *(might get sick, to get dry)*

3. Why does the server at a restaurant give you a bill? *(so you know how much to pay for your food)*

4. How do you heat food in the microwave? *(put it in a microwave dish, cover it, set the time, and press "Start")*

5. How could someone lose weight? *(exercise, eat healthy, avoid fatty foods)*

6. How do you know what time a certain TV program is on? *(TV Guide, newspaper, cable listing)*

7. Why does a police car have a siren? *(to warn drivers to pull over, to let people know there's an emergency)*

8. Why might the lifeguard at a swimming pool blow her whistle and yell, "Stop!"? *(Someone is doing something that's against the rules.)*

9. Why shouldn't you open someone else's mail? *(not polite, doesn't belong to you)*

10. How do computers help us at school? *(Answers will vary.)*

11. Why is it better to recycle things than to throw them away? *(helps protect the environment)*

12. How long should you wait for someone to answer the door when you knock? *(Answers will vary.)*

13. Why do some people get a new car? *(They want to, The old one is broken.)*

14. How can you find out what the weather is before you get dressed? *(listen to the radio, watch the news, look or go outside)*

15. How do you know if a store is open? *(doors are unlocked, people are inside, look at hours posted on the window, call first)*

16. Why do our interests change as we get older? *(We like different things at different ages.)*

Answering Questions 5

Say, "Listen to each question. Picture both things in your mind and think of how they are the same. Then answer the question."

1. How are a book and a newspaper the same? *(can read both, both have words, both have stories)*

2. How are a bed and a couch the same? *(both furniture, can lie down on both, both are soft)*

3. How are a bike and a motorcycle the same? *(can ride both, both have two wheels, both have handlebars)*

4. How are a chair and a bench the same? *(both furniture, can sit on both, both have a seat and a back)*

5. How are a lion and a horse the same? *(both animals, both have manes, both have tails)*

6. How are an eagle and an airplane the same? *(both have wings, both fly)*

7. How are a radio and a CD player the same? *(both play music, both can be plugged in)*

8. How are a goldfish and a whale the same? *(both live in water, both swim)*

9. How are a carrot and an orange the same? *(both are food, both are orange)*

10. How are a watch and a clock the same? *(both tell time)*

11. How are soap and detergent the same? *(both are used to get something clean)*

12. How are tape and glue the same? *(both are sticky, both hold things together)*

13. How are fingers and toes the same? *(both are body parts, 10 of each)*

14. How are a tire and a donut the same? *(both are round, both have a hole in the middle)*

15. How are a cloud and a pillow the same? *(both can be white, both can be fluffy)*

16. How are a baseball cap and a football helmet the same? *(both worn on your head, both worn for sports)*

17. How are blue and green the same? *(both are colors)*

18. How are a tree and a bush the same? *(both are plants, both grow, both have leaves, both have branches)*

19. How are sandals and tennis shoes the same? *(both worn on your feet, both are kinds of shoes, both can be made of leather)*

20. How are a fan and an air conditioner the same? *(both keep you cool, both need electricity to run)*

Comparisons

100% Listening – Intermediate

22

Answering Questions 6

Say, "Listen to each question. Picture both things in your mind and think of how they are different. Then answer the question."

1. How are a bicycle and a tricycle different? *(bicycle has two wheels; tricycle has three wheels)*

2. How are a sock and a shoe different? *(sock is made of cloth, wear it under your shoe; shoe is made of leather, wear it over your sock)*

3. How are milk and ice cream different? *(milk is liquid, you drink it; ice cream is solid, you eat it)*

4. How are a kitten and a puppy different? *(kitten is a cat; puppy is a dog)*

5. How are a tiger and a leopard different? *(tiger has stripes; leopard has spots)*

6. How are water and ice different? *(water is liquid; ice is frozen water)*

7. How are a stove and a refrigerator different? *(stove heats food; refrigerator cools food)*

8. How are a box and a jar different? *(box made of cardboard, can't see through it; jar made of glass or plastic, can see through it)*

9. How are a bookstore and a library different? *(buy books at bookstore; borrow books from library)*

10. How are a street and a sidewalk different? *(cars drive on streets; people walk on sidewalks)*

11. How are a fork and a spoon different? *(fork has tines/prongs, use it to eat solid foods; use spoon to eat liquid foods)*

12. How are a necklace and a bracelet different? *(wear necklace around neck; wear bracelet around wrist)*

13. How are a towel and a washcloth different? *(towel larger than a washcloth, use towel to dry yourself; use washcloth to wash yourself)*

14. How are gloves and mittens different? *(gloves have places for thumb and each finger; mittens have one place for thumb and one place for all fingers)*

15. How are rings and earrings different? *(wear rings on fingers/toes; wear earrings in ears)*

16. How are letters and numbers different? *(use letters to make words; use numbers to count)*

17. How are a pillow and a blanket different? *(pillow soft, put your head on it; blanket warm, cover your body with it)*

18. How are a skirt and pants different? *(skirt doesn't have legs; pants have legs)*

19. How are a door and a window different? *(walk through door; look through window)*

20. How are a lion and a house cat different? *(lion is wild; house cat is tame)*

Answering Questions 7

Say, "Answer these questions to give your opinion."

(Note: Answers will vary.)

1. Which activity would you rather do, go swimming or go sledding?

2. Do you like or dislike getting up early in the morning?

3. Who do you think is better at playing video games, you or your best friend?

4. Which would you rather watch on TV, sports or cartoons?

5. Which sport do you like better, ice hockey or basketball?

6. Would you rather ride in, a canoe or a speedboat?

7. Which would you rather eat for breakfast, pancakes or cereal?

8. Would you rather read a book or watch a movie on TV?

9. Do you think our lunch period is too short, too long, or just right?

10. Would you rather learn about astronauts or inventors?

11. Do you enjoy going on long trips in the car or do you think it's boring?

12. Who should get to choose what to serve in the cafeteria every day, the cooks or the students?

13. What is your favorite kind of pizza?

14. What is your favorite game to play outside?

15. What animal would you most like to have for a pet?

16. Where would you most like to go on vacation?

17. What time do you think you should go to bed at night?

18. If you break something that doesn't belong to you, what should you do?

19. Do you think recycling is important or a waste of people's time?

20. How long do you think kids should be allowed to talk on the telephone at one time?

21. Do you think it should be a law that people must wear helmets when riding a motorcycle?

22. Who do you think is the most important player on a baseball team?

Answering Questions 8

Say, "Answer these questions to give your opinion."

(Note: Answers will vary. To make the task easier, do not require students to tell why.)

1. What movie do you think everyone should see? Why?

2. Do you like helping take care of younger children? Why?

3. How many times a day should you brush your teeth? Why?

4. Do you think teachers should have to take tests too? Why?

5. Would you rather talk on the phone to your friend or E-mail her? Why?

6. Do you think magician's tricks are real? Why?

7. What is the best time to do your homework? Why?

8. Would you rather spend the night at a friend's house or have the friend stay at your house? Why?

9. What is one school rule you'd like to change? Why?

10. Who do you like to talk to when you have a problem? Why?

11. Do you think all people in vehicles should have to wear seatbelts? Why?

12. Do you think it's important to have a computer in every classroom? Why?

13. Do you think the school day is too long, not long enough, or just right? Why?

14. Should young children be allowed to watch scary movies? Why?

15. What should you do if you find something that doesn't belong to you? Why?

16. Do you think it's a good idea to drink soda with every meal? Why?

17. Is it ever okay to tell a lie? Why?

18. Do you think we should have curfews for kids under 16? Why?

19. What should happen to someone who gets caught cheating on a test? Why?

20. What should you do if you get a letter in the mail that doesn't belong to you? Why?

21. What activity don't you like to do at school? Why?

22. What is the name of a TV show you don't enjoy watching? Why?

Answering Questions 9

Say, "I'm going to tell you some problems. After each problem I will give you two possible solutions. Tell me which solution best solves the problem."

1. Dylan can't find his lunch money in his backpack. What should he do?
    *   take someone else's lunch money out of their backpack
    *   *(ask someone if he can borrow some money for lunch)*

2. Lily forgot to tell her dad that she had basketball practice after school. Lily's dad is waiting outside to pick her up. What should Lily do?
    *   *(go to the car to tell her dad she has practice)*
    *   go to basketball practice

3. Martin didn't finish his book report that's due today. Instead of working on it last night, he went over to a friend's house to play. What should he say to his teacher?
    *   *(I apologize. May I have an extra day to finish my report?)*
    *   I finished my report, but I lost it on the way to school.

4. Mr. Montero said some mean things to his neighbor. Now his neighbor won't speak to him. What should Mr. Montero do?
    *   *(apologize to his neighbor)*
    *   ignore his neighbor

5. Tanya's alarm clock broke last week and she's been late to school ever since. What should Tanya do?
    *   stay awake all night
    *   *(ask someone she lives with to wake her up on time)*

6. Jared's mom told him to pack his bag for the football game before going to bed last night, but Jared didn't listen. Now Jared is late for the game and he can't find his uniform. What should he do?
    *   wear what he has on to the game
    *   *(keep looking for his uniform as quickly as he can, ask someone to help him look)*

Answering Questions 10

Say, "Listen to each situation. Then answer my questions."

1. Someone is calling to talk to Roberto's mom. Roberto doesn't know who it is.
   What is Roberto's problem? *(He doesn't know who's on the phone.)*
   What should Roberto do? *(Ask the person, "Who's calling?")*

2. Josie just got new glasses. She needs them to see the chalkboard. When Josie was reading her book, she took her glasses off. Now she can't find them.
   What is Josie's problem? *(She can't find her glasses.)*
   What should Josie do? *(Answers will vary.)*

3. Michael forgot to wear his raincoat or bring his umbrella to school today. It's raining out when school gets over, and Michael has to walk home.
   What is Michael's problem? *(It's raining and he forgot his raincoat and umbrella.)*
   What should Michael do? *(Answers will vary.)*

4. Ricky is waiting for his mom to get home from work. He's hungry, but he knows he isn't supposed to have a snack this close to dinnertime.
   What is Ricky's problem? *(He's hungry, but he's not supposed to snack before dinner.)*
   What should Ricky do? *(Answers will vary.)*

5. Courtney walked barefoot to her friend's house across the street. While she was walking, she stepped on a piece of glass and cut her foot.
   What is Courtney's problem? *(She cut her foot on some glass.)*
   What should Courtney do? *(Answers will vary.)*

6. Cynthia was watching TV after school when a news bulletin came on that said there's a tornado warning for her area.
   What is Cynthia's problem? *(There's a tornado warning for her area.)*
   What should Cynthia do? *(take cover until the warning is over)*

Answering Questions 11

Say, "Answer these questions."

(Note: Answers will vary.)

1. When wouldn't you wear sunglasses?

2. What wouldn't you do if you missed the bus after school?

3. How wouldn't you talk to your parent or another adult?

4. What kind of animal wouldn't make a good pet?

5. When wouldn't someone go to the dentist's office?

6. How wouldn't you say hi to your best friend?

7. Where wouldn't you like to go for a birthday party?

8. What is something you can't buy at a grocery store?

9. What is one shape that doesn't have curved sides?

10. How wouldn't you act if you got an *A* on your math quiz?

11. When wouldn't you go to school?

12. What is something you wouldn't wear to school?

13. Where wouldn't you look if you couldn't find your shoes?

14. Why doesn't a bandage help a broken leg get better?

15. What is one animal that doesn't walk on four legs?

16. What wouldn't you see during a baseball game?

17. When wouldn't you watch TV?

18. What wouldn't you do if you know the answer to your teacher's question?

19. Where wouldn't be a good place to play?

20. What shouldn't you use a musical instrument for?

21. How wouldn't you talk during a movie at the theater?

22. When wouldn't you congratulate someone?

Exclusion

Answering Questions 12

Say, "Answer these questions."

(Note: Answers will vary. To make the task easier, do not require students to tell why.)

1. When might a person not want to go out to eat? Why?

2. When wouldn't a person frown? Why?

3. What wouldn't you do to earn money to buy a new bicycle? Why?

4. Where wouldn't you want to go with a friend? Why?

5. How wouldn't you answer the telephone? Why?

6. When wouldn't you wear shorts? Why?

7. Where wouldn't you go on a rainy day? Why?

8. Where wouldn't a person go if she were sick? Why?

9. What wouldn't you wear to bed at night? Why?

10. What is something you shouldn't do at school? Why?

11. Where wouldn't a person take her vehicle to get it cleaned? Why?

12. How wouldn't you carry a new puppy? Why?

13. What food wouldn't you eat if you were hungry? Why?

14. When wouldn't you plant flowers outside? Why?

15. What is a sport that doesn't use a ball? Why?

16. When wouldn't people shiver? Why?

17. Where wouldn't be a good place to walk barefoot? Why?

18. When wouldn't you eat lunch in the school cafeteria? Why?

19. What ingredient wouldn't you put on a sandwich? Why?

20. Where wouldn't you hang a picture of your family? Why?

21. When wouldn't a person use a flashlight? Why?

22. What kind of music don't you like to listen to? Why?

Exclusion

Following Directions

Following directions requires good listening and logical thinking skills. For success in school, it is critical that students be able to accurately follow oral directions. In this unit, students will follow directions with a variety of exercises such as:

- determining if a statement is a direction

- determining if a direction makes sense

- doing activities described

- drawing items described

- changing a sentence so it means the opposite

- solving math problems

- performing conditional directions

- identifying items described

Extension Activities

Read a story aloud to your students. Choose a word in the story that recurs several times. Have students raise their hands or clap each time they hear the word.

Set up a barrier between two students. Give each student the same set of blocks or objects. Have one student arrange the blocks any way he chooses. Then have that student describe how his blocks are arranged for the other student. Encourage the student who is listening to ask questions as she arranges her blocks. Then compare the arrangements.

Following Directions 1

Say, "Listen to each sentence. Raise your hand if the sentence is a direction."

1. Our teacher was sick today. *(no)*

2. Write your name at the top of the paper. *(yes)*

3. Count the hands of everyone who will ride the bus tomorrow. *(yes)*

4. We had a spelling test today. *(no)*

5. Raise your hand if you have a question. *(yes)*

6. Maddie broke her arm. *(no)*

7. Read the first ten pages of the book. *(yes)*

8. Look in the table of contents to see what page Chapter 4 starts on. *(yes)*

9. The rainbow didn't last long after the storm. *(no)*

10. Logan left his backpack on the bus. *(no)*

11. Add the numbers in the column and write the answer below the line. *(yes)*

12. After you read the story, answer the questions on the bottom of the page. *(yes)*

13. Stand up quickly and line up at the door in single file. *(yes)*

14. Amanda went to the science museum on Saturday. *(no)*

15. Choose a country to do your presentation on. *(yes)*

16. We played the music loudly. *(no)*

17. Jack wrote a short story about life on Mars. *(no)*

18. Use the dictionary to look up any words you don't know how to spell. *(yes)*

19. Read all of the directions before you begin. *(yes)*

20. Explain why the main character helped the king. *(yes)*

Following Directions 2

Say, "Some of these directions make sense; some of them don't. Listen carefully to each direction. If it makes sense, raise your hand."

1. Give me the window. *(no)*

2. Don't walk on the grass. *(yes)*

3. Jump over the building. *(no)*

4. Please hang up your jacket. *(yes)*

5. Put the milk in the stove. *(no)*

6. Help me carry the school. *(no)*

7. Count to 20 as fast as you can. *(yes)*

8. Draw a picture on the moon. *(no)*

9. Wash your hands before you eat. *(yes)*

10. Take your backpack home. *(yes)*

11. Ride your bike in the lake. *(no)*

12. Play the piano with your hair. *(no)*

13. Stand on your head under the table. *(no)*

14. Tell me your phone number. *(yes)*

15. Throw your foot in the trash. *(no)*

16. Wipe your muddy boots on the mat. *(yes)*

17. Read the first two chapters in this book. *(yes)*

18. Open the floor. *(no)*

19. Brush your teeth with ketchup. *(no)*

20. Turn the computer off when you are finished. *(yes)*

Following Directions 3a & 3b

Following Directions 3a

Give each student a copy of page 34. Then read the following directions.

Say, "You'll need a pencil to do this activity. Listen carefully. Look at the pictures and follow the directions."

1. Draw in the clock hands to show what time school starts in the morning. *(Answers will vary.)*

2. Solve both of the math problems on the chalkboard. *(31, 15)*

3. Write the name of your favorite book on the book cover. *(Answers will vary.)*

4. Write the month of your birthday in the box at the top of the calendar. Then circle the day of your birthday. *(Answers will vary.)*

5. Draw a square around the food you would most like to eat. Put an X on the food you would least like to eat. *(Answers will vary.)*

Following Directions 3b

Give each student a copy of page 35. Then read the following directions.

Say, "You'll need a pencil to do this activity. Listen carefully and follow the directions."

1. Look at Box 1. Cross out the name that is more than one syllable. *(Stephanie)*

2. Look at Box 2. Skip the first two numbers. Then circle the third number. *(60)*

3. Look at Box 3. Fill in the blank with a word that makes sense. *(Answers will vary.)*

4. Look at Box 4. Underline all the words that rhyme with *bear*. *(share, where, pear)*

5. Look at Box 5. Circle the list of words that is in alphabetical order. *(heart, lungs, stomach)*

6. Look at Box 6. Write the longest word you can think of in this box. *(Answers will vary.)*

7. Look at Box 7. Rewrite these sentences using the correct capitalization and punctuation. *(Amber said, "My party is tomorrow. I hope you can come.")*

Use this page with the directions on page 33.

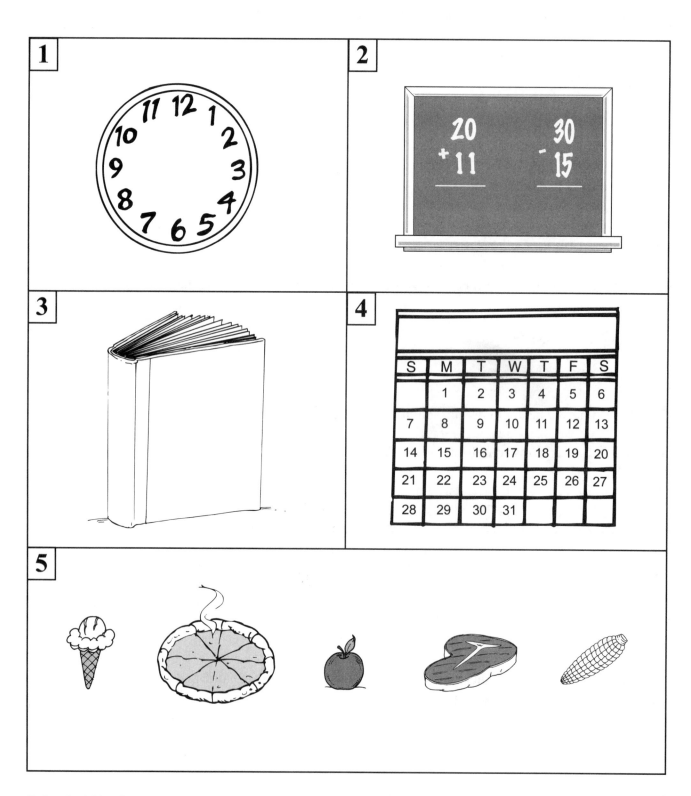

1

2

20
+ 11

30
- 15

3

4

S	M	T	W	T	F	S
	1	2	3	4	5	6
7	8	9	10	11	12	13
14	15	16	17	18	19	20
21	22	23	24	25	26	27
28	29	30	31			

5

Following Directions 3b

Use this page with the directions on page 33.

1

    Brooke   Max   Stephanie

2

   22   44   60   75   99

3

   Tyler found a _____ in his backpack.

4

   share   dear   where   pear

5

heart	den	microscope
lungs	cave	telescope
stomach	ocean	periscope

6

7

   amber said my party is tomorrow I hope you can come

Following Directions 4

Say, "A grid helps you find places and things on a map. A grid is made of squares. The squares that go up and down make columns. Each column has a letter. Look at this grid. Column C is shaded." (Show students the grid.)

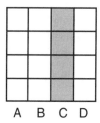

Say, "The squares that go across make rows. Each row has a number. Look at this grid. Row 4 is shaded." (Show students the grid.)

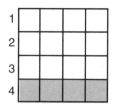

Say, "The letters and numbers name the squares. Look at this grid. The shaded square is in column C and row 4. The name of this square is C4." (Show students the grid.)

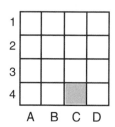

Give each student a copy of page 37. Then read the following directions.

Say, "You'll need a pencil to do this activity. Listen carefully. Look at the map and follow the directions."

1. Draw a store in square B3.

2. Draw a pond in square C2.

3. Draw a house in square A4.

4. Draw a swing set in square E1.

5. Draw trees in the rest of the blank squares.

Use this page with the directions on page 36.

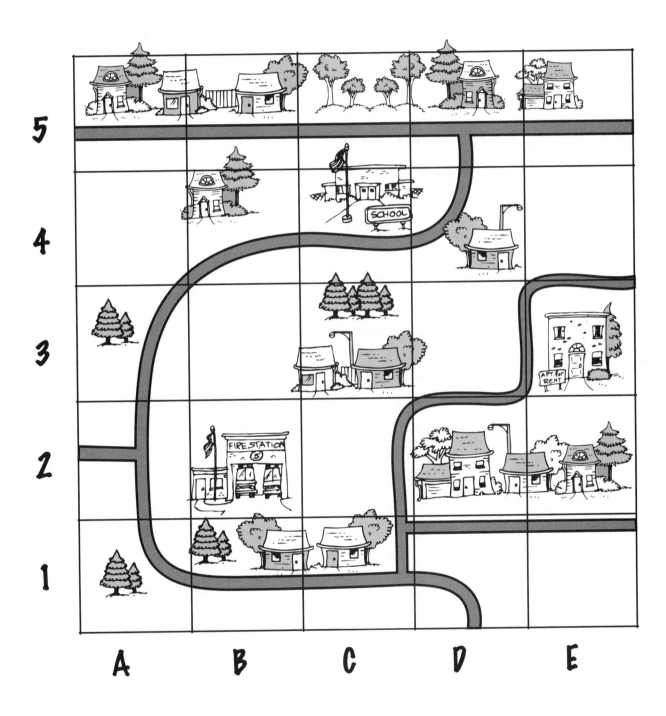

Following Directions 5

Say, "I'll say a word. Then I'll use that word in a sentence. You repeat the sentence, but use a word that means the opposite of the word I used. For example, I say, '**Hot** – The soup was hot.' The opposite of *hot* is *cold*, so you would answer, 'The soup was cold.'"

1. **easy** – The spelling test was really easy. *(The spelling test was really hard.)*

2. **first** – Kelsey was the first one in line. *(Kelsey was the last one in line.)*

3. **left** – We turned left to go to the park. *(We turned right to go to the park.)*

4. **dangerous** – It's dangerous to cross this bridge. *(It's safe to cross this bridge.)*

5. **deep** – The water in the pond was deep. *(The water in the pond was shallow.)*

6. **wide** – John walked down the wide hallway. *(John walked down the narrow hallway.)*

7. **straight** – The sidewalk was straight. *(The sidewalk was crooked/curved.)*

8. **smooth** – All of the rocks were smooth. *(All of the rocks were rough/bumpy.)*

9. **north** – We walked north to find the cave. *(We walked south to find the cave.)*

10. **sharp** – The knife was sharp. *(The knife was dull.)*

11. **begin** – We were ready for the party to begin. *(We were ready for the party to end.)*

12. **late** – Brian was late for school. *(Brian was early for school.)*

13. **before** – Nicole read the story before recess. *(Nicole read the story after recess.)*

14. **forward** – Erin moved forward so she wouldn't be in the way. *(Erin moved backward so she wouldn't be in the way.)*

Following Directions 6

Say, "Listen carefully. Solve these math problems."

Addition		**Multiplication**	
1. 10 + 20 *(30)*	11. 100 + 41 *(141)*	1. 10 x 5 *(50)*	11. 7 x 7 *(49)*
2. 40 + 15 *(55)*	12. 60 + 25 *(85)*	2. 11 x 4 *(44)*	12. 33 x 3 *(99)*
3. 20 + 20 *(40)*	13. 50 + 55 *(105)*	3. 9 x 4 *(36)*	13. 100 x 1 *(100)*
4. 35 + 20 *(55)*	14. 11 + 88 *(99)*	4. 9 x 9 *(81)*	14. 20 x 3 *(60)*
5. 44 + 44 *(88)*	15. 15 + 15 *(30)*	5. 6 x 7 *(42)*	15. 25 x 4 *(100)*
6. 75 + 25 *(100)*	16. 70 + 14 *(84)*	6. 5 x 5 *(25)*	16. 8 x 10 *(80)*
7. 30 + 33 *(63)*	17. 75 + 75 *(150)*	7. 8 x 8 *(64)*	17. 22 x 2 *(44)*
8. 50 + 27 *(77)*	18. 42 + 62 *(104)*	8. 6 x 6 *(36)*	18. 50 x 2 *(100)*
9. 10 + 85 *(95)*	19. 31 + 59 *(90)*	9. 5 x 9 *(45)*	19. 30 x 3 *(90)*
10. 45 + 45 *(90)*	20. 28 + 47 *(75)*	10. 4 x 4 *(16)*	20. 8 x 100 *(800)*

Subtraction		**Division**	
1. 75 – 25 *(50)*	11. 50 – 25 *(25)*	1. 25 ÷ 5 *(5)*	11. 60 ÷ 3 *(20)*
2. 50 – 10 *(40)*	12. 45 – 35 *(10)*	2. 40 ÷ 2 *(20)*	12. 49 ÷ 7 *(7)*
3. 100 – 80 *(20)*	13. 66 – 33 *(33)*	3. 80 ÷ 8 *(10)*	13. 100 ÷ 4 *(25)*
4. 88 – 44 *(44)*	14. 100 – 20 *(80)*	4. 36 ÷ 6 *(6)*	14. 45 ÷ 5 *(9)*
5. 20 – 20 *(0)*	15. 95 – 70 *(25)*	5. 100 ÷ 2 *(50)*	15. 70 ÷ 2 *(35)*
6. 65 – 30 *(35)*	16. 150 – 50 *(100)*	6. 50 ÷ 5 *(10)*	16. 44 ÷ 2 *(22)*
7. 48 – 28 *(20)*	17. 82 – 40 *(42)*	7. 66 ÷ 11 *(6)*	17. 75 ÷ 3 *(25)*
8. 70 – 60 *(10)*	18. 49 – 19 *(30)*	8. 32 ÷ 4 *(8)*	18. 90 ÷ 10 *(9)*
9. 85 - 30 *(55)*	19. 99 – 44 *(55)*	9. 28 ÷ 7 *(4)*	19. 56 ÷ 7 *(8)*
10. 60 – 15 *(45)*	20. 58 – 22 *(36)*	10. 81 ÷ 9 *(9)*	20. 63 ÷ 7 *(9)*

Following Directions 7

Say, "Listen carefully to these directions. Wait until you hear all the directions before you start."

1. If you have a sister, put your right hand in the air. If you don't have a sister, put your left hand in the air.

2. If you have blue eyes, cover them with your hands. If you don't have blue eyes, cover your ears.

3. If your last name starts with a vowel, stand up. If your last name doesn't start with a vowel, hold your nose.

4. If you have a dog, clap your hands twice. If you don't have a dog, fold your hands in your lap.

5. If you have blue on, blink your eyes. If you don't have blue on, wave goodbye.

6. If you wear glasses, raise both hands. If you don't wear glasses, touch your chin.

7. If you have socks on, touch your socks. If you don't have socks on, say "No."

8. If you like peanut butter and jelly sandwiches, say "Yes." If you don't like peanut butter and jelly sandwiches, cover your mouth.

9. If your hair is brown, put your hands on your head. If you don't have brown hair, touch your nose.

10. If you were born in this state, stand up and turn around. If you weren't born in this state, name the state where you were born.

11. If your birthday is in summer, act like you're really hot. If your birthday isn't in summer, say when your birthday is.

12. If you are the oldest child in your family, look up at the ceiling. If you are not the oldest child in your family, look down at the floor. If you have no brothers or sisters, shake your head "No."

Following Directions 8

Give each student a copy of page 42. Then read the following directions.

Say, "You'll need some colored pencils or markers to do this activity. Listen carefully. I'll give you clues about a state. Color each one I describe."

1. I am a state in the West. The Pacific Ocean is on one side of me. Many people came here to find gold in the 1800s. I'm one of the biggest states. Disneyland is here. Color me yellow. *(California)*

2. It's very warm here most of the time. Many fruits, like pineapples and coconuts, grow here. You have to fly or take a boat to get here. I'm the only state made up of islands. Color me orange. *(Hawaii)*

3. I'm in the Midwest. I'm called the Buckeye State. Many U.S. Presidents were born here. Michigan and Lake Erie border me on the north. Color me blue. *(Ohio)*

4. I am in New England. The Atlantic Ocean is on one side of me. Paul Revere made his famous ride here. My capital is Boston. Color me green. *(Massachusetts)*

5. I'm in the South. The Atlantic Ocean is one one side of me, and the Gulf of Mexico is on the other side of me. There are many tourist attractions here. Color me red. *(Florida)*

6. I'm in the Southwest. The Gulf of Mexico borders me on the east. I'm one of the biggest states. Color me purple. *(Texas)*

7. Not many people live here because it's cold most of the time. I'm one of the biggest states. My capital is Juneau. Color me brown. *(Alaska)*

8. I am in the Northeast. I am the smallest state. Color me any color you like. *(Rhode Island)*

Following Directions 8, continued

Use this page with the clues on page 41.

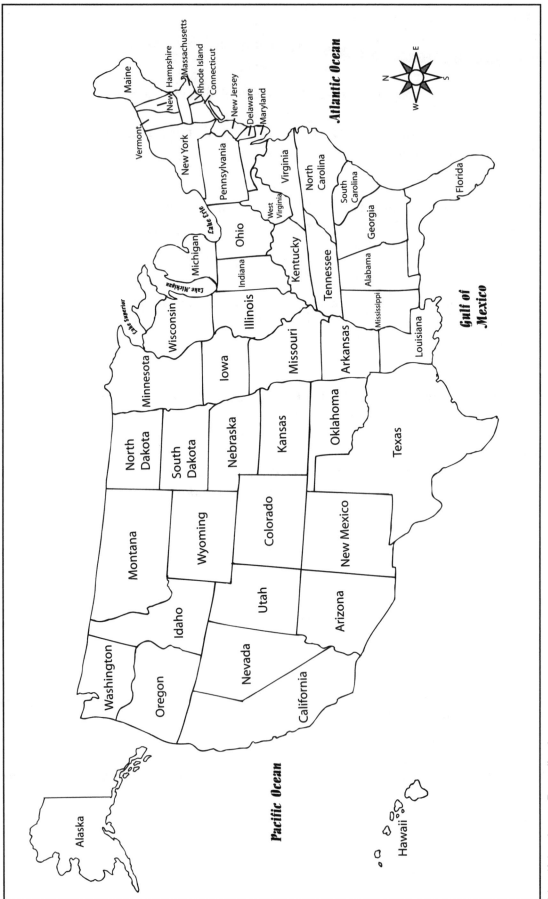

Identifying Items Described
100% Listening – Intermediate

Categories

When students understand the concept of categorization, they are better able to make sense of the world. Making connections by recognizing similarities is an important thinking skill and a building block that leads to higher critical thinking.

In this unit, your students will practice categorization from a variety of perspectives. As you work through these activities, encourage your students to consider these factors when dealing with lists of information that might be categorized:

- Have them consider the similarities among items. How are a dog and a cat alike?
  (They are both animals, they both have fur, and they could both be pets.)
  As you add more items to consider, the similarities might broaden or narrow.

- Have them consider the differences between items or groups. How are a dog, a cat, and a lion alike or different?
  (They are all animals. They are all fur-covered. Two of them make good pets and the other is a wild animal.)

What are the characteristics and functions of items students are exploring? What sensory details might the items have in common? What are the items used for? Where do you find them? Answering these questions will allow your students to either place items in a category or decide they don't belong together at all.

Placing items in categories and naming categories allows students to test their personal hypotheses and lets them set up their own rules to define their environment.

Categories 1

Give each student a copy of page 45. Say, "Things in categories are related in some ways and different in others. Listen carefully. I'll tell you a word in the category *school subjects*. Then I'll tell you some information about that word. Look at the diagram and tell me which box each piece of information I give you belongs in."

1. math
   - learn addition, subtraction, multiplication, division *(what is learned)*
   - used when taking a test, shopping, playing games *(when it's used)*
   - used by scientists, accountants, parents, teachers *(who uses it)*
   - learn to survive in life and in jobs *(why learn it)*
   - used especially in places where you pay for things *(where it's used)*

2. social studies
   - learn to understand how people interact *(why learn it)*
   - used by sociologists, psychologists, and counselors *(who uses it)*
   - learn about cultures, beliefs, and religions *(what is learned)*
   - used in every location to understand how people behave *(where it's used)*
   - used whenever there's something new to figure out *(when it's used)*

3. science
   - learn about how all of nature works *(what is learned)*
   - learn about ourselves and our environment *(why learn it)*
   - used in hospitals, laboratories, parks, etc. *(where it's used)*
   - used by medical personnel, scientists, and researchers *(who uses it)*
   - used whenever there are nature problems that need solutions *(when it's used)*

4. reading and literature
   - used during 70% of your waking hours *(when it's used)*
   - used by everyone to gain information or for pleasure *(who uses it)*
   - used wherever something is printed: books, newspapers, magazines, billboards, instruction manuals, store signs, etc. *(where it's used)*
   - need to know what's going on in the world *(why learn it)*
   - learn how to sound out words and understand what you read *(what is learned)*

5. English
   - learn about grammar, punctuation, and the rules of writing *(what is learned)*
   - used whenever writing is necessary *(when it's used)*
   - used by everyone to know how to communicate in writing *(who uses it)*
   - used anywhere you need to communicate in writing *(where it's used)*
   - learn other ways to communicate besides talking *(why learn it)*

Use this diagram with the prompts on page 44.

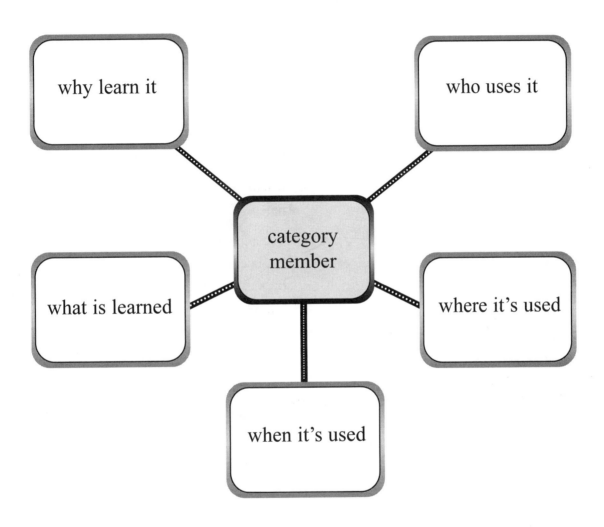

Categories 2

Give each student a copy of page 47. Say, "Your worksheet has six categories on it: Math, Science, American History, Social Studies, English, and Art. Listen carefully. I'll tell you some words. You write the words on the line under the correct category."

(Note: Deliver the words randomly, alternating groups, to test students' abilities to listen for the appropriate category. As you read each item, put a check in the box next to it. This will help you keep track of the items you've already given to the students.)

Math

- ☐ addition
- ☐ subtraction
- ☐ multiplication tables
- ☐ division

Science

- ☐ biology
- ☐ anatomy
- ☐ zoology
- ☐ anthropology

American History

- ☐ Pilgrims
- ☐ slavery
- ☐ Civil War
- ☐ Spanish-American War

Social Studies

- ☐ Industrial Revolution
- ☐ cultures
- ☐ early transportation
- ☐ technology revolution

English

- ☐ capitalization
- ☐ punctuation
- ☐ book report
- ☐ novel

Art

- ☐ painting
- ☐ sculpture
- ☐ pottery
- ☐ color wheel

Use this page with the prompts on page 46.

Math

1. _____

2. _____

3. _____

4. _____

Social Studies

1. _____

2. _____

3. _____

4. _____

Science

1. _____

2. _____

3. _____

4. _____

English

1. _____

2. _____

3. _____

4. _____

American History

1. _____

2. _____

3. _____

4. _____

Art

1. _____

2. _____

3. _____

4. _____

Categories 3

Give each student a copy of page 49. Say, "You use your five senses in school every day, all day. I'll say some words. You tell me which sense category each word belongs to. Write the word I say under the correct heading or headings. Remember that some words may use more than one of your senses."

(Note: As you read each item, put a check in the box next to it. This will help you keep track of the items you've already given to the students.)

☐ paste *(smell or taste, touch)*
☐ pencil *(touch)*
☐ playground *(sound)*
☐ water fountain *(smell or taste, touch)*
☐ gym *(smell or taste, sound)*
☐ pencil sharpener *(sound)*

☐ computer mouse *(touch)*
☐ birthday treats *(smell or taste)*
☐ scissors *(sound, touch)*
☐ cafeteria *(smell or taste, sound)*
☐ locker room *(smell or taste, sound)*
☐ finger paints *(touch)*

Finished answer sheet should read:

Smell or Taste	Sound	Touch
1. paste	1. playground	1. paste
2. water fountain	2. gym	2. pencil
3. gym	3. pencil sharpener	3. water fountain
4. birthday treats	4. scissors	4. computer mouse
5. cafeteria	5. cafeteria	5. scissors
6. locker room	6. locker room	6. finger paints

Categories 3, *continued*

Name _____

Use this page with the prompts on page 48.

Smell or Taste

1. _____
2. _____
3. _____
4. _____
5. _____
6. _____

Sound

1. _____
2. _____
3. _____
4. _____
5. _____
6. _____

Touch

1. _____
2. _____
3. _____
4. _____
5. _____
6. _____

Identifying Categories and Their Members
100% Listening – Intermediate

Categories 4

Give each student a copy of page 51. Say, "There are many different nouns. Look at the chart and write each word I say under the correct heading."

(Note: As you read each item, put a check in the box next to it. This will help you keep track of the items you've already given to the students.)

☐ forest *(common noun)*
☐ sailors *(plural noun)*
☐ kings *(plural noun)*
☐ Henry Hudson *(proper noun)*
☐ President Bush *(proper noun)*
☐ teacher *(common noun)*
☐ river *(common noun)*
☐ Isabel *(proper noun)*
☐ feet *(plural noun)*
☐ Aunt Betty *(proper noun)*
☐ hot dogs *(plural noun)*
☐ queen *(common noun)*
☐ October *(proper noun)*
☐ alligators *(plural noun)*
☐ Egypt *(proper noun)*

☐ pencil *(common noun)*
☐ mice *(plural noun)*
☐ carpenter *(common noun)*
☐ Ms. Okawa *(proper noun)*
☐ month *(common noun)*
☐ grandparents *(plural noun)*
☐ daughter *(common noun)*
☐ Mississippi River *(proper noun)*
☐ boats *(plural noun)*
☐ vice presidents *(plural noun)*
☐ president *(common noun)*
☐ map *(common noun)*
☐ Statue of Liberty *(proper noun)*
☐ explorers *(plural noun)*
☐ George Washington *(proper noun)*

Finished answer sheet should read:

Proper Noun	Common Noun	Plural Noun
1. Henry Hudson	1. forest	1. sailors
2. President Bush	2. teacher	2. kings
3. Isabel	3. river	3. feet
4. Aunt Betty	4. queen	4. hot dogs
5. October	5. pencil	5. alligators
6. Egypt	6. carpenter	6. mice
7. Ms. Okawa	7. month	7. grandparents
8. Mississippi River	8. daughter	8. boats
9. Statue of Liberty	9. president	9. vice presidents
10. George Washington	10. map	10. explorers

Categories 4, *continued*

Name _____

Use this page with the prompts on page 50.

Proper Noun

1. _____

2. _____

3. _____

4. _____

5. _____

6. _____

7. _____

8. _____

9. _____

10. _____

Common Noun

1. _____

2. _____

3. _____

4. _____

5. _____

6. _____

7. _____

8. _____

9. _____

10. _____

Plural Noun

1. _____

2. _____

3. _____

4. _____

5. _____

6. _____

7. _____

8. _____

9. _____

10. _____

Identifying Categories and Their Members
100% Listening – Intermediate

Categories 5

Say, "There are three different verb tenses: present, past, and future. We use the present tense when we're talking about what's happening right now. We use the past tense when we talk about what happened before now. We use the future tense when we're talking about what will happen later. I'll say a sentence. You tell me if it's about the present, past, or future."

1. My favorite ice cream flavor is Rocky Road. *(present)*

2. Are you going to tell Mom I came home late? *(future)*

3. As the bell rang, we bolted out the door. *(past)*

4. Karen wishes I would finish talking on the phone! *(present)*

5. Tyler decided to play baseball instead of cutting the grass. *(past)*

6. Send the money to me for your ticket. *(present)*

7. These crackers will get stale quickly. *(future)*

8. My English teacher gave me an A+ on this paper. *(past)*

9. This boomerang won't come back when I throw it. *(present)*

10. The turtle eggs will hatch in 60 to 80 days. *(future)*

11. My computer isn't working. *(present)*

12. Everyone came to the party except Bruce. *(past)*

13. Will you be over soon? *(future)*

14. I think I'll go skiing this winter. *(future)*

15. I'm doing my homework. *(present)*

16. The school Olympics will start on Monday. *(future)*

17. Kim was the star of the school play. *(past)*

18. We drove to the Grand Canyon last summer. *(past)*

Categories 6

Say, "The United States is made up of 50 states. Each state belongs to one of these regions: Northeast, Southeast, Midwest, Southwest, Western, and Pacific Coast. Listen as I name each of the 50 states. You tell me which region it belongs to."

(Note: To help your students, list the categories on the chalkboard and use the United States map on page 42 as a visual aide for this activity. Before beginning, explain that the Mason-Dixon Line which separates Pennsylvania from Maryland is considered the dividing line between the Northeast and the Southeast states.)

1. Nebraska *(Midwest)*
2. Alaska *(Pacific Coast)*
3. New York *(Northeast)*
4. Florida *(Southeast)*
5. Missouri *(Midwest)*
6. Mississippi *(Southeast)*
7. California *(Pacific Coast)*
8. Iowa *(Midwest)*
9. New Hampshire *(Northeast)*
10. Wyoming *(Western)*
11. West Virginia *(Southeast)*
12. Alabama *(Southeast)*
13. Connecticut *(Northeast)*
14. Colorado *(Western)*
15. Illinois *(Midwest)*
16. South Carolina *(Southeast)*
17. New Mexico *(Southwest)*
18. Delaware *(Southeast)*
19. Tennessee *(Southeast)*
20. Ohio *(Midwest)*
21. Nevada *(Western)*
22. Pennsylvania *(Northeast)*
23. Oklahoma *(Western)*
24. South Dakota *(Midwest)*
25. Vermont *(Northeast)*
26. Arizona *(Southwest)*
27. Indiana *(Midwest)*
28. Maryland *(Southeast)*
29. Louisiana *(Southeast)*
30. Minnesota *(Midwest)*
31. Michigan *(Midwest)*
32. Kentucky *(Southeast)*
33. Hawaii *(Pacific Coast)*
34. Utah *(Western)*
35. Washington *(Pacific Coast)*
36. Texas *(Southwest)*
37. Maine *(Northeast)*
38. Georgia *(Southeast)*
39. Kansas *(Midwest)*
40. Idaho *(Western)*
41. North Carolina *(Southeast)*
42. North Dakota *(Midwest)*
43. Oregon *(Pacific Coast)*
44. Virginia *(Southeast)*
45. Massachusetts *(Northeast)*
46. Arkansas *(Southeast)*
47. Wisconsin *(Midwest)*
48. Montana *(Western)*
49. Rhode Island *(Northeast)*
50. New Jersey *(Northeast)*

Categories 7

Say, "Listen carefully. I'm going to read you a list of words. One of the words doesn't belong with the others. Tell me what that word is. Then tell me what category the rest of the words belong to."

(Note: As an added challenge, have students name one more member of each category.)

1. hamster, elephant, goldfish, dog *(elephant; pets)*

2. Vermont, Illinois, Mexico, Montana *(Mexico; U.S. states)*

3. ant, grasshopper, beetle, snake *(snake; bugs/insects)*

4. rock 'n' roll, trumpet, hip hop, country *(trumpet; types of music)*

5. spring, rain, snow, sleet *(spring; types of weather/precipitation)*

6. notebook, monitor, mouse, keyboard *(notebook; parts of a computer)*

7. dollar, pound, peso, check *(check; currency/money)*

8. Atlantic, Pacific, Indian, Mississippi, Arctic *(Mississippi; oceans)*

9. pen, paste, pencil, marker, chalk *(paste; things you write with)*

10. sports, news, sitcoms, orchestra, documentary *(orchestra; things you watch on TV)*

11. couch, lantern, tent, sleeping bag *(couch; camping equipment)*

12. page, index, author, cover, spine *(author; parts of a book)*

13. broccoli, asparagus, cauliflower, watermelon, potato *(watermelon; vegetables)*

14. equator, northeast, southwest, east, northwest *(equator; directions)*

15. submarine, ship, sailboat, rowboat, subway *(subway; types of water transportation)*

16. push-ups, jumping jacks, sit-ups, somersaults, knee bends *(somersaults; exercises)*

17. Chicago, Minneapolis, Illinois, Pittsburgh, Orlando *(Illinois; U.S. cities)*

18. football, referee, soccer, downhill skiing, softball *(referee; sports)*

19. lungs, heart, kidneys, skin, foot *(foot; body organs)*

20. lemonade, coffee, iced tea, fruit juice, soda pop *(coffee; cold drinks)*

Categories 8

Say, "I'm going to give you the name of a category. Then I'll read you a paragraph about that category. Listen closely for all the words that go with the category. When I finish the paragraph, you tell me all the category members I said."

1. The category is fruits and vegetables.
   I asked Mr. Evans if he had any apples or pears today. He told me he just received a shipment of apples and sweet corn today, but no pears. I decided to get peaches instead. I also picked up some green beans.

   (apples, pears, sweet corn, peaches, green beans)

2. The category is things at a grocery store.
   Every Saturday morning I go with my father to the grocery store. We push a shopping cart up and down the aisles. We fill the cart with everything on our shopping list. Then we go to the checkout counter. The cashier checks out our groceries and puts them into plastic bags.

   (shopping cart, aisles, shopping list, checkout counter, cashier, groceries, plastic bags)

3. The category is things in a restaurant.
   I set my menu down on the table and looked around. What was I going to have? I played with the napkin holder for a few seconds. The server came over to take our orders. All I could think about was what I was going to have for dessert!

   (menu, table, napkin holder, server, orders, dessert)

4. The category is things at an amusement park.
   We had a great time on vacation. We went to an amusement park. I rode the smallest roller coaster. It was so much fun! Dad would only ride the merry-go-round. He did eat a lot of popcorn though. My little sister liked the shows. She saw some of her favorite cartoon characters.

   (roller coaster, merry-go-round, popcorn, shows, cartoon characters)

5. The category is things in a school gym.
   We like rainy days. That means we get to have recess in the gym. We have to wear our gym shoes so we don't ruin the wood floor. The place is filled with flying basketballs. Some people are rolling around on scooters. Others are playing with jump ropes. There are a few kids just sitting on the bleachers and reading. Recess in the gym is always noisy and exciting.

   (gym shoes, wood floor, basketballs, scooters, jump ropes, bleachers)

Riddles

Answering riddles requires students to evaluate information and make judgments about what they hear. As students answer these riddles, they'll strengthen their listening skills as well as improve vocabulary and naming skills. In addition, they will sharpen their thinking skills as they narrow down choices to guess the object described in the riddle.

Have the student listen to the riddle and guess the object. The first clue is general so students can think of many possible choices. You might want to write them down. The second clue helps narrow down the choices more. The third clue should give the student the information needed to guess the answer to the riddle.

Items progress in difficulty.

Riddles 1

Say, "Listen to each clue I give. Then tell me what you think I'm describing."

1. This is in a classroom or library.
    It's a big book.
    It tells you how to spell words.
    (dictionary)

2. This is part of a book.
    It's found near the front of the book.
    It shows you the page numbers of the
       chapters.
    (table of contents)

3. It's a big bird.
    It has a long neck and long, skinny legs.
    It cannot fly, but it runs very fast.
    (ostrich)

4. It is a big building.
    Many people go there.
    It has many stores in it.
    (mall)

5. It flies.
    It goes into outer space.
    It lands on a runway like an ordinary plane.
    (space shuttle)

6. It's a big country.
    It's in North America.
    It's north of the United States.
    (Canada)

7. It covers a large area.
    Many animals live in it.
    It's a large body of salt water.
    (ocean)

8. It's a continent.
    It's far away from the United States.
    Koalas and kangaroos live there.
    (Australia)

9. It's a form of transportation.
    It moves slowly.
    People traveled this way when they went
       west in the 1800s.
    (covered wagon, horse and carriage)

10. It belongs to the cat family.
    It lives in the jungle.
    It has spots.
    (cheetah, leopard)

11. This is an opening in the earth's surface.
    It makes a rumbling noise.
    Lava and smoke come out of the top of it.
    (volcano)

12. You plug it in.
    It has several different parts to it.
    It has a mouse attached to it.
    (computer)

13. This has buttons on it.
    You hold it in your hand.
    You use it with a TV to change the channels.
    (remote control)

14. It's an animal.
    It lives in the woods.
    It's black and white and has a bad smell.
    (skunk)

Riddles 2

Say, "Listen to each clue I give. Then tell me what you think I'm describing."

1. It goes on your head.
   It's made of hard plastic.
   It protects your head when you ride your bike.
   (helmet)

2. It's a game.
   It's played with two teams on a field.
   Each team tries to kick the ball into the goal.
   (soccer)

3. You see this at an amusement park.
   You ride it.
   You go up and down hills really fast.
   (roller coaster)

4. This has a zipper.
   You use it when you go camping.
   You get in it when you want to go to sleep.
   (sleeping bag, tent)

5. It's a bird.
   It's colorful.
   It can talk.
   (parrot)

6. This usually happens during warm weather.
   It can be dangerous.
   It's called a funnel cloud.
   (tornado)

7. They're made of metal and plastic.
   They go in your mouth.
   They make your teeth straight.
   (braces, retainer)

8. This is made of leather.
   It holds money.
   Men carry it in their back pocket.
   (wallet)

9. You usually find this in a library.
   It's used for research.
   It's a set of books with lots of information.
   (encyclopedia)

10. It's a piece of furniture.
    You see it in an office or in a child's room.
    You sit at it and study or work.
    (desk)

11. You look through this.
    Scientists use it.
    It helps you see things far away.
    (telescope)

12. This uses electricity.
    It's found in homes and cars.
    You use it to play music.
    (tape player, CD player, radio)

13. This is a very large animal.
    It lives in Africa.
    It's part of the monkey family.
    (gorilla)

14. You can hold this in your hands.
    You can look through it.
    It uses film.
    (camera)

Riddles 3

Say, "Listen to each clue I give. Then tell me what you think I'm describing."

1. It's a big bird.
   It doesn't fly.
   It's often eaten on Thanksgiving.
   (turkey)

2. You mostly see this in big cities.
   It's a vehicle.
   It's a train that runs underground.
   (subway)

3. This is a big animal.
   You usually see it in the desert.
   It has one or two humps.
   (camel)

4. This goes in the sky.
   People ride in it.
   People stand in a basket as it goes up.
   (hot air balloon)

5. This has numbers on it.
   It's found in a doctor's office.
   You use it to measure temperature.
   (thermometer)

6. You use this to measure things.
   It's made of wood.
   It's three feet long.
   (yardstick)

7. You use these in winter.
   They go on your feet.
   You slide down a hill wearing them.
   (skis)

8. These open and close.
   They are made of fabric.
   They hang in front of windows.
   (curtains)

9. It's a planet.
   It's far from the Sun.
   It's the smallest planet.
   (Pluto)

10. You see this in the sky.
    It doesn't last very long.
    You see it after it rains if the Sun is out.
    (rainbow)

11. This is used by hikers and explorers.
    You hold it in your hand.
    It shows North, South, East, and West.
    (compass, map)

12. It's a plant.
    It doesn't need much water to grow.
    It's found in a desert.
    (cactus)

13. This has wheels.
    You push it.
    It's used to cut grass.
    (lawn mower)

14. There are many of these in the United States.
    People go there to learn.
    Many teenagers go there when they finish
      high school.
    (college/university)

Riddles 4

Say, "Listen to each clue I give. Then tell me what you think I'm describing."

1. These are part of your body.
   You have two of them.
   They help you breathe.
   (lungs)

2. This is a musical instrument.
   It's a brass instrument.
   It has a part that you slide back and forth.
   (trombone)

3. You use these when you eat.
   They can be made of wood or plastic.
   People use them when they eat Chinese food.
   (chopsticks)

4. People speak Spanish in this county.
   Many people live there.
   It's directly south of the United States.
   (Mexico)

5. This is a type of animal.
   They live on land.
   Snakes, lizards, and turtles are this kind of
     animal.
   (reptile)

6. This is hot during the day and cold at night.
   It's a place that gets very little rain.
   It's covered in sand.
   (desert)

7. This is part of a house.
   You have to go down some stairs to get to it.
   It's also called a cellar.
   (basement)

8. This is a form of punctuation.
   It goes at the end of a sentence.
   You use it when you ask a question.
   (question mark)

9. This is a kind of boat.
   It only holds two or three people.
   You use oars to paddle it.
   (canoe, rowboat)

10. This place has many plants and animals.
    It's very warm there.
    It rains a lot.
    (rain forest)

11. This is made of metal.
    It's a tool.
    You use it to tighten nuts.
    (wrench)

12. This is made of plastic.
    It's a child's toy.
    You put it around your waist and move your
      hips to make it go around.
    (hula hoop)

13. These are part of your body.
    They are inside you.
    They make up your skeleton.
    (bones)

14. He was President of the United States.
    He lived in the 1800s.
    He helped end slavery.
    (Abraham Lincoln)

Riddles 5

Say, "Listen to each clue I give. Then tell me what you think I'm describing."

1. This is a big body of water.
    Many boats travel up and down it.
    It's the longest river in the United States.
    (Mississippi River)

2. This place has sand all around it.
    There are palm trees and water on it.
    It's found in a desert.
    (oasis)

3. This can be found in warm or cold places.
    You can only get there by airplane or boat.
    It's land surrounded by water.
    (island)

4. He was a great leader in the U.S. Army.
    He was President of the United States.
    He was the first President.
    (George Washington)

5. This animal lives in the woods.
    It only comes out at night.
    It has quills to protect itself.
    (porcupine)

6. This is a form of punctuation.
    It goes at the end of a sentence.
    It means you're excited about something.
    (exclamation point)

7. This country is in Europe.
    It's part of an island.
    The United States declared its independence
       from this country in 1776.
    (Great Britain, England)

8. You see this on a globe.
    It's very far away.
    It's at the top of the world.
    (North Pole)

9. This is found on mountains.
    It moves very slowly.
    It's a huge mass of ice.
    (glacier)

10. This is a natural disaster.
    It brings a lot of rain and very high winds.
    It's also called a tropical storm.
    (hurricane)

11. This is found in outer space.
    It's made of ice, dust, and rock.
    It has a long, glowing tail.
    (comet)

12. This is a unit of time.
    You measure it with a calendar.
    It's the same as 12 months.
    (year)

13. These were built thousands of years ago.
    They are made of big blocks of limestone.
    They are found in Egypt.
    (pyramids)

14. This is an animal.
    Part of its life is spent in the water and part is
       spent on land.
    It hops.
    (frog, toad)

Riddles 6

Say, "Listen to each clue I give. Then tell me what you think I'm describing."

1. You look through this.
    Scientists use it.
    It helps you see very small things up close.
    (microscope)

2. It's on a map.
    It's an imaginary line.
    It divides the Earth in half horizontally.
    (equator)

3. You find these on a boat.
    They float.
    People wear them to be safe.
    (life jackets/life vests)

4. This is a kind of rock.
    It's extremely hot.
    It comes from an erupting volcano.
    (lava)

5. This is found in outer space.
    It makes a bright streak through the sky.
    It's also called a shooting star.
    (meteor)

6. This is a famous landmark.
    It's in Massachusetts.
    The Pilgrims landed here when they first came
        over from England.
    (Plymouth Rock)

7. This often comes in the mail.
    It's a small card.
    It asks you to come to a party.
    (invitation)

8. This happened in the 1800s.
    Abraham Lincoln was the President.
    It was the war between the states.
    (The Civil War)

9. You see this on a map.
    It's usually in a box.
    It's a list of the symbols found on the map.
    (legend/key)

10. You see this at a circus.
    Acrobats hold on to it.
    It swings back and forth in the air.
    (trapeze)

11. This is a hot spring of water.
    It shoots boiling water and steam into the air.
    A famous one is called Old Faithful.
    (geyser)

12. This book tells a true story.
    It tells all about a person's life.
    The author is the person in the story.
    (autobiography)

13. This is a way to communicate.
    You use your hands.
    People who are deaf or hard of hearing use
        this to "talk."
    (sign language)

14. This is a family member.
    This person is older than you.
    He is your mom's father.
    (grandfather)

Riddles 7

Say, "Listen to each clue I give. Then tell me what you think I'm describing."

1. This is a kind of story.
    It explains historical events.
    It often has gods and goddesses in it.
    (myth)

2. This is found on an envelope.
    It's part of the address.
    It's numbers that identify the city and state.
    (zip code)

3. This person uses a telescope.
    This person is a scientist.
    This person studies the solar system.
    (astronomer)

4. This is a major part of United States history.
    It gave freedom to people.
    It was signed on July 4, 1776.
    (The Declaration of Independence)

5. This happens in outer space.
    It doesn't happen very often.
    It's the partial or complete covering of the
       moon or Sun.
    (eclipse)

6. This is part of your body.
    It's in your neck.
    It's the tube that allows food to go into your
       stomach.
    (esophagus)

7. This animal lives in Australia.
    The mother carries its baby in a pouch on her
       belly.
    This animal looks like a small bear.
    (koala)

8. This person was an inventor.
    He taught people who were deaf.
    He invented the telephone.
    (Alexander Graham Bell)

9. This is like a magazine.
    It has lots of pictures in it.
    People order things out of it.
    (catalog)

10. You have two of these on your body.
    They are on your head.
    You breathe air through them.
    (nostrils)

11. This is long and flat.
    Two or three people can sit on it.
    You use it to slide down snowy hills.
    (toboggan)

12. This is a weather condition.
    When it happens it's hard to see.
    It happens when clouds are close to the
       ground.
    (fog)

13. This is in Central America.
    It took a long time to build.
    It allows ships to easily pass from the
       Atlantic Ocean to the Pacific Ocean.
    (Panama Canal)

14. This is a large bird.
    It has webbed feet.
    It uses the pouch on its bill to catch fish.
    (pelican)

Asking Questions for Comprehension

Students may have difficulty understanding oral information for a variety of reasons. Sometimes it's because they are simply poor listeners. Other times it's due to the fact that they lack the skills necessary to identify the important information in a message. However, sometimes it has nothing to do with the listener at all, but rather, the message itself is unclear. These vague or unclear messages can confuse students and interfere with active listening.

Many educators believe that active listening is one of the most important skills students need in order to be successful. Active listeners are able to identify vague or confusing information and ask the appropriate questions to clarify what they have not understood. This unit teaches students to identify the need to clarify as well as how to ask for clarification appropriately. Students will use thinking and language skills to listen critically to information and watch the speaker carefully for gestures that may be critical to understanding the message.

The importance of good oral communication skills will be stressed as students:

- identify vague information
- explain why some messages are unclear
- ask questions to clarify vague messages

When presenting these lessons to a group, some of the items that are intended to be clear communications may appear unclear because no definite person is indicated (e.g., The direction *Say your name* is clear when it is intended for one person). To avoid confusion, call on individual students for these items.

Asking Questions for Comprehension 1

Say, "Some directions are hard to follow because the speaker doesn't explain what to do very clearly. For example, I might tell you to 'Look over there,' but unless I point to a certain place, you don't know where 'there' is.

"Listen to these directions. Watch me carefully while I'm talking. If you understand exactly what to do, give me a 'thumbs up' like this (demonstrate). If you don't understand exactly what to do, give me a 'thumbs down' like this (demonstrate)."

(*Note:* Y *indicates* "thumbs up." N *indicates* "thumbs down.")

1. Hold up three fingers. *(Y)*

2. Put your homework here when you are finished. [Point somewhere.] *(Y)*

3. Wave to that person. *(N)*

4. Tell me what this is called. [Point to a body part.] *(Y)*

5. Name two teachers at this school. *(Y)*

6. Color this one green and that one blue. *(N)*

7. Look up that word in the dictionary and write its definition. *(N)*

8. Take out a sheet of paper and write your name at the top. *(Y)*

9. Clap your hands and then stand over here. [Point somewhere.] *(Y)*

10. Go to the back of the room and then face that way. *(N)*

11. Tell me what this is and then show me how to use it. *(N)*

12. Say the days of the week and then tell me what day it is today. *(Y)*

13. Will you please find out what time it starts? *(N)*

14. Add any three numbers and then divide the sum by two. *(Y)*

15. Show me how you look when you feel this way. *(N)*

16. Subtract three from five and then whisper the answer. *(Y)*

17. After you stand up, tell me where you put them. *(N)*

18. Draw one and then circle it with a red marker. *(N)*

19. Take out your book and read this paragraph aloud. *(N)*

20. Please hand me that before you sit down. [Point to something.] *(Y)*

21. Tell me an animal that lives in Africa and then cover your ears. *(Y)*

22. Please tell her that he's looking for her. *(N)*

23. Before you take a book home, be sure to check it out of the library. *(Y)*

24. Pick those up and put them over here. *(N)*

Asking Questions for Comprehension 2

Say, "Some directions are hard to follow because the speaker doesn't explain what to do very clearly. Listen to these directions. Watch me carefully while I'm talking. If you understand exactly what to do, then do it. If you don't understand exactly what to do, say 'I'm not sure what to do.'"

1. Meet me there after recess. *(I'm not sure what to do.)*

2. Pretend to answer the phone and talk to your best friend.

3. [Hold up a book.] Tell me what this is and then stand next to the door.

4. Name two girls' names that begin with that letter. *(I'm not sure what to do.)*

5. Name something in this room that is made of plastic.

6. Pretend you're showing her how to use it. *(I'm not sure what to do.)*

7. Tell me what shape and size that is. *(I'm not sure what to do.)*

8. Tell me the name of your favorite computer game and how to play it.

9. Go find one on my desk and bring it to me. *(I'm not sure what to do.)*

10. [Point to something.] Can you tell me what this is?

11. After you stand up, bend over and touch the floor.

12. Think of a three-syllable word and then say it while clapping the syllables.

13. Say it loudly and then say it softly. *(I'm not sure what to do.)*

14. Please walk over there and then come back. *(I'm not sure what to do.)*

15. Name the odd numbers on the clock and then tell me your favorite animal.

16. Say the word *laughter* and then show me what it means.

17. Take off your right shoe and put it under there. *(I'm not sure what to do.)*

18. Tear it in half. Then crumple up both pieces and put them in the trash. *(I'm not sure what to do.)*

19. Point to something in this room and then tell me what color the item is.

20. [Point to one of the child's hands.] Count the fingers on that hand and then hold your breath for three seconds.

21. Tell me what you would say if that happened. *(I'm not sure what to do.)*

22. Describe how you feel when you go there. *(I'm not sure what to do.)*

Asking Questions for Comprehension 3

Say, "Some messages are unclear because the speaker doesn't give you enough information. Listen carefully to each message I say. Then answer my questions."

1. Lauri told Donna her mom was waiting for them in front of the school.
   Do you know whose mom is waiting? *(no)*
   Is the message clear or unclear? *(unclear)*

2. If you're in a building when the fire alarm goes off, immediately go to the nearest exit and go outside.
   Do you know where to go if the fire alarm goes off in a building? *(yes)*
   Is the message clear or unclear? *(clear)*

3. Jim and John were talking about the baseball game. Jim told John he hit a home run in the third inning.
   Do you know who hit the home run? *(no)*
   Is this message clear or unclear? *(unclear)*

4. Half of the people in Libby's class want to make puppets for art, but the other half want to make masks. Libby wants to make them too.
   Do you know what Libby wants to make? *(no)*
   Is this message clear or unclear? *(unclear)*

5. Dave wants everyone to meet at his house tonight. He said not to be late.
   Do you know what time to be at Dave's house? *(no)*
   Is this message clear or unclear? *(unclear)*

6. Roosevelt School has a strict policy about smoking. Any student caught smoking cigarettes will be expelled.
   Do you know what will happen to students who get caught smoking? *(yes)*
   Is this message clear or unclear? *(clear)*

7. School milk prices will go up next week. Please remember to bring the correct amount for milk next week.
   Do you know how much milk will cost next week? *(no)*
   Is this message clear or unclear? *(unclear)*

Asking Questions for Comprehension 4

Say, "Listen to these unclear directions. Tell why each is hard to follow."

(Note: Encourage students to be specific. For an added challenge, ask students to identify two reasons the direction is unclear in items 12-18.)

1. Pretend you just found one. *(I don't know what "one" is.)*

2. Remind her to call you after school. *(I don't know who to remind.)*

3. Name something you can buy there. *(I don't know where you mean.)*

4. Take out a sheet of paper and write each one three times. *(I don't know what to write.)*

5. Cover your eyes with them. *(I don't know what to cover my eyes with.)*

6. Can you give me directions to their house? *(I don't know whose house.)*

7. Open your reading book to page 56 and read the sentence aloud. *(I don't know which sentence to read.)*

8. Get the broom and the dustpan out of the closet. Then give them to her. *(I don't know who to give them to.)*

9. Finish your book report and then write your spelling words two times. When you're finished, put your work over there. *(I don't know where to put my work.)*

10. Write your name in the top right corner of your paper and the date in the top left corner. Then underline it. *(I don't know what to underline.)*

11. Take out your crayons and put them on your desk. Pick up that crayon when I say "now." [Pause.] Now. *(I don't know which crayon to pick up.)*

12. If you'd like to do that after school, clap your hands this many times. *(I don't know what "that" is or how many times to clap.)*

13. Please share yours with her. *(I don't know what to share or who to share with.)*

14. Get one and put it over there. *(I don't know what to get or where to put it.)*

15. You should ask him where it is. *(I don't know who to ask or what I'm asking about.)*

16. If your eyes are this color, stand over there. *(I don't know what color you're talking about or where to stand.)*

17. Tell her what time it starts. *(I don't know who to tell or what "it" is.)*

18. Pretend you're showing her how to make them. *(I don't know who to show or what "them" is.)*

Asking Questions for Comprehension 5

Say, "Listen to these directions. Watch me carefully while I'm talking. If you understand exactly what to do, then do it. If you don't understand what to do, say 'I'm not sure what to do.' Then tell me why my direction is unclear."

1. Take out your math book and do problems 1-10. *(I'm not sure what to do. I don't know which page to turn to.)*

2. Wave at me and then pretend to take my picture.

3. Walk over to the door and knock on it three times.

4. Color the triangle crimson. *(I'm not sure what to do. I don't know what color "crimson" is.)*

5. Tell me what you use to do this. [Pantomime brushing teeth.] *(toothbrush, toothpaste)*

6. Point to something in this room that is that color. *(I'm not sure what to do. I don't know what color you're talking about.)*

7. Show me where you put it. *(I'm not sure what to do. I don't know what "it" is.)*

8. After I count to five, stand up and face that way. [Pause.] One, two, three, four, five. *(I'm not sure what to do. I don't know which way to face.)*

9. Stand up, bend over, and touch your toes with both hands.

10. Look around the room. When you find one, raise your hand. *(I'm not sure what to do. I don't know what to look for.)*

11. Tell me which of these things you would see there: fork, sink, garden, light bulb. *(I'm not sure what to do. I don't know where "there" is.)*

12. Listen to these words: camera, ruler, paint, ribbon. Tell me what the last word was.

13. Tell me how many letters are in his first name. *(I'm not sure what to do. I don't know whose name you're talking about.)*

14. Pretend to fold your paper in half and then do this. [Pantomime putting something in a drawer.]

15. Point to where she sits after you stand over here. [Point somewhere.] *(I'm not sure what to do. I don't know who "she" is.)*

16. Before you hand it to me, do this. [Scratch your head.] *(I'm not sure what to do. I don't know what to hand to you.)*

Asking Questions for Comprehension 6

Say, "Some messages are hard to understand. The speaker knows what he wants to tell you, but he doesn't explain it very well. Listen carefully to each message. Then answer my questions."

1. Madelyn and her dad went to Dairy Delight to get a treat. Madelyn told the woman behind the counter that she would like an ice-cream cone.
   Is this message clear or unclear? *(unclear)*
   Why? *(The woman doesn't know what flavor or size ice-cream cone Madelyn wants.)*

2. Beau's dad called your brother to tell him that he has the flu. Your brother worked on homework at Beau's house last night, so he might get the flu too.
   Is this message clear or unclear? *(unclear)*
   Why? *(I don't know whether Beau or his dad has the flu.)*

3. The recipe said to drop small spoonfuls of the cookie batter onto a greased cookie sheet. Then bake the cookies at 350 degrees for 12 minutes.
   Is this message clear or unclear? *(clear)*

4. Because of the heat, baseball practice will end early. Be sure to tell your parents to pick you up on time.
   Is this message clear or unclear? *(unclear)*
   Why? *(It doesn't say what time baseball practice will end.)*

5. Grant Elementary students are having a hunger drive. Please help by bringing canned goods or other non-perishable food items.
   Is this message clear or unclear? *(unclear)*
   Why? *(It doesn't say where or when to bring the food items.)*

6. The bookmobile comes once a week. Remember to bring your library card so you can check out some books.
   Is this message clear or unclear? *(unclear)*
   Why? *(It doesn't say where or when the bookmobile comes.)*

7. Soccer sign-up will be tomorrow after school in the gym. Please bring a signed permission slip from your parents.
   Is this message clear or unclear? *(clear)*

Asking Questions for Comprehension 7

Give each student a copy of page 72. Then read the following directions.

Say, "You'll need a pencil to do this activity. Look at your worksheet. Listen carefully to the directions I give you. If you understand exactly what to do, then do it. If you don't understand exactly what to do, tell me why my direction is hard to follow."

1. Copy the word in the star on line number 1. *(I don't know which star.)*

2. Copy the word in the middle star on line number 1. *(long)*

3. Point to the first triangle. Write that word on line number 2. *(tree)*

4. Point to the word on top. Copy it on line number 3. *(I don't know which word on top to point to.)*

5. Point to the shape above the last star. Copy the word in it on line number 3. *(the)*

6. On line number 4, copy the word that's in the circle. *(I don't know which circle.)*

7. Look at the bottom row of shapes. Copy the last word in that row on line number 4. *(cold)*

8. Find the word in the first circle. Copy it on line number 5. *(run)*

9. Write that word on line number 6. *(I don't know which word to write.)*

10. Look at the stars. Copy the word you see on line number 6. *(I don't know which word to copy.)*

11. Look at this star. [Point to the last star.] Write this word on line number 6. *(ball)*

12. I want you to write that word on line number 7. *(I don't know which word to write.)*

13. Look at the center circle. Write that word on line number 7. *(you)*

14. If it's in one of the stars, write it on line number 8. *(I don't know which word in the star to write.)*

15. Find the word in a star that means *a few*. Write it on line number 8. *(some)*

16. Find the word with the letter "l" in it. Copy it on line number 9. *(Three of the words have an "l" in them.)*

17. Look at the word you wrote on line number 3. Write it again on line number 9. *(the)*

18. Point to the middle shape on the bottom row. Copy that word on line number 10. *(sit)*

Finished answer sheet should read:

1.	long	6.	ball
2.	tree	7.	you
3.	the	8.	some
4.	cold	9.	the
5.	run	10.	sit

Use this page with the directions on page 71.

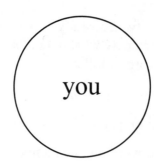
run

you

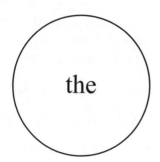
the

some

long

ball

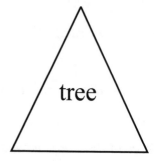
tree

sit

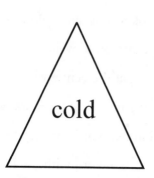
cold

1. _____

2. _____

3. _____

4. _____

5. _____

6. _____

7. _____

8. _____

9. _____

10. _____

Asking Questions for Comprehension 8

Say, "Some directions are hard to follow. Listen carefully to each direction. Then answer my questions to help you understand it."

(Note: For an added challenge, ask students to identify two reasons the direction is unclear in items 5 and 6.)

1. Tell me what the answer is.
   Why is this direction unclear? *(I don't know what the question is.)*
   What question could you ask? *(What is the question?)*

2. Draw a flag, a sun, and a clock. Then color that one.
   Why is this direction unclear? *(I don't know which picture "that one" is.)*
   What question could you ask? *(Which picture should I color?)*

3. Put an X in the blank that precedes the correct answer.
   Why is this direction unclear? *(I don't know what "precedes" means.)*
   What question could you ask? *(What does "precede" mean?)*

4. Submit your entries for the poetry contest by Thursday afternoon.
   Why is this direction unclear? *(I don't know who to give my entry to.)*
   What question could you ask? *(Who do I submit my entry to?)*

5. Please tell him to get me one too.
   Why is this direction unclear? *(I don't know who you want me to tell or what you want me to tell him to get you.)*
   What questions could you ask? *(Who should I tell? What do you want him to get you?)*

6. Don't forget to put it in there before it starts to rain.
   Why is this direction unclear? *(I don't know what to put in or where exactly to put it.)*
   What questions could you ask? *(What do you want me to put in before it rains? Where do you want me to put it?)*

Asking Questions for Comprehension 9

Say, "Some messages are unclear because the speaker doesn't give you enough information. Listen carefully to each message. Then answer my questions to help you understand it."

(Note: For an added challenge, ask students to identify two reasons the message is unclear in item 6.)

1. Joan told Jennifer that her handwriting is hard to read.
    Why is this message unclear? *(I don't know whether Joan's handwriting or Jennifer's handwriting is hard to read.)*
    What question could you ask? *(Is Joan's or Jennifer's handwriting hard to read?)*

2. Mrs. Harris said that if it ever happens again we won't be able to use paints for our art projects anymore.
    Why is this message unclear? *(I don't know what happened.)*
    What question could you ask? *(What shouldn't we do anymore?)*

3. Calvin said not to go to that movie because it's too boring.
    Why is this message unclear? *(I don't know what movie Calvin is taking about.)*
    What question could you ask? *(Which movie do you mean, Calvin?)*

4. Mr. Grant's fourth-grade students should meet there after lunch. The principal wants to congratulate them for selling the most school calendars.
    Why is this message unclear? *(I don't know where the students should meet.)*
    What question could you ask? *(Where should we meet after lunch?)*

5. Jack told Phil he wouldn't be able to play kickball during recess today. Miss Flores wants him to help put up the new bulletin board.
    Why is this message unclear? *(I don't know whether Jack or Phil won't be able to play kickball.)*
    What question could you ask? *(Who won't be able to play at recess?)*

6. Isabel's birthday party is this Saturday. Please let her know if you can come.
    Why is this message unclear? *(I don't know where or what time the party is.)*
    What questions could you ask? *(Where is the party? What time does it start and when will it be over?)*

Asking Questions for Comprehension 10

Say, "Some directions are unclear because the speaker doesn't tell you exactly what to do. Listen to each direction and tell whether it's clear or unclear. If it's unclear, tell me a question you could ask to find out exactly what to do."

1. Listen as I read some sentences. Circle the one that goes with the sentence you hear.
   (unclear; What should I circle?)

2. When you've finished your story, exchange your paper with a partner. Proofread your partner's story and correct any spelling or punctuation errors.
   (clear)

3. Before starting your art project, solve the problems in your math book. Explain how you found each answer.
   (unclear; What page are the problems on?)

4. Circle and underline the nouns and the verbs in these sentences.
   (unclear; Which should I circle and which should I underline?)

5. Take out a sheet of paper and write this week's spelling words in alphabetical order. Then use each word in a sentence.
   (clear)

6. Leave the papers on my desk until he gets here. Then put them in this drawer. [Point.]
   (unclear; Who should I wait for before putting the papers in the drawer?)

7. Find six items in the classroom to measure that are shorter than your ruler. Measure each item and record your findings in the chart on page 66 of your math workbook.
   (clear)

8. Have each player choose a token, place it at Start, and roll the die. That person goes first. Play continues to the left.
   (unclear; Who goes first?)

9. Spread newspaper on your work area. Place three of them on your newspaper. Label them **A**, **B**, and **C**, with a different letter for each one.
   (unclear; What should I put on my newspaper and label?)

Asking Questions for Comprehension 11

Say, "Some messages are unclear because the speaker doesn't give you enough information. Listen to each message and tell whether it's clear or unclear. If the message is unclear, tell me a question you could ask to find out the missing information."

1. I won't be at school because my family is going on vacation. Please send my homework assignments home with Jeff.
   (unclear; When will you be gone?)

2. On your way home, please stop at the store and pick up a gallon of milk, a loaf of bread, and two packages.
   (unclear; What should I get two packages of?)

3. Spirit Day will be this Thursday. Be sure to wear the school T-shirt your teacher gave you last week.
   (clear)

4. There will be a book fair this Tuesday during lunch. If you want to go, you need to tell her today.
   (unclear; Who should I tell if I want to go to the book fair?)

5. Please take it out of the freezer when you get home from school. At 4:30, heat the oven to 350 degrees and put it in. When I get home, we'll eat it for dinner.
   (unclear; What should I take out of the freezer?)

6. I told Mr. Jenkins you could baby-sit Saturday night from 7:00-11:00. He said he would pick you up at 6:45 at your house.
   (clear)

7. A ring was found in one of the girls' rest rooms today. Come to the front office to claim it. You'll need to describe the ring in detail.
   (clear)

8. Mrs. Burrows will be our guest speaker today. Write one question you'd like to ask her about her career after she's finished speaking.
   (unclear; What does Mrs. Burrows do?)

9. Please remember to sign the get-well card for Mr. Wong before leaving today. He'll be back at school tomorrow, and we'll give him the card during lunch.
   (unclear; Where should I go to sign the card?)

Asking Questions for Comprehension 12

Materials: Each student needs a red, blue, brown, yellow, orange, and green crayon; a pencil; and a copy of page 78.

Say, "Look at the picture on your worksheet. I'm going to give you some directions that go with it. Listen carefully. If you understand exactly what to do, then do it. If you don't understand exactly what to do, ask me a question to help you."

1. Color it blue. *(What should I color blue?)* Color the water blue.

2. Look at the lake. Draw a thing in the water. *(What should I draw in the water?)* Draw a boat in the water.

3. Pick up your yellow crayon.

4. Use your yellow crayon to draw one of those in the sky. *(What should I draw in the sky?)* Draw a yellow sun in the sky.

5. Pick up your pencil. Draw a hat on her head. *(Which person do you mean?)* Draw a hat on the girl who is running.

6. After you color the umbrella green, color the lighthouse red.

7. Pick up that crayon and color the boat you drew. *(Which crayon should I use?)* [Point to a crayon.] Use that crayon to color the boat.

8. Pick up your pencil and draw a cloud here. [Point somewhere on the worksheet.]

9. Use your orange crayon to make one of those in between the children on the beach. *(What should I make?)* Make a ball with your orange crayon.

10. Color the beach brown.

11. If you see it, use your pencil to draw a line from the lighthouse to it. *(What do you want me to draw a line to?)* Draw a line from the lighthouse to the dock.

12. Using your pencil, draw a person fishing off of the dock.

13. Tell me what she is doing. *(Whom do you mean?)* Tell me what the mom is doing.

14. Use this color crayon to draw a fish in the water near the dock. [Point to a crayon.]

15. Now hang your picture over there. *(Where should I hang my picture?)* [Point to a place in your room.] Hang your picture there.

Asking Questions for Comprehension 12, *continued*

Name _____

Use this page with the directions on page 77.

Asking Questions for Clarification
100% Listening – Intermediate

Paraphrasing

Paraphrasing is a good skill to introduce to primary students. Paraphrasing will be beneficial to them as they receive directions, relay conversations, or simplify information.

Here are some specific strategies for paraphrasing:

- **Use Synonyms**

  Some information your students receive may contain large, complicated words. Have your students replace these words with smaller words. For instance, they might replace the word *inexpensive* with *cheap*. Make sure your students understand that if they substitute one word for another, they must use a correct synonym. If they don't, they may accidentally change the meaning of the information.

- **Use Only Important Information**

  Help your students determine what information is vital and what information can be left out. This will help them reduce the number of words they have to remember.

- **Use Step-by-Step Words**

  Have your students paraphrase directions or sequential information by using words such as *first, next, then, after that, second,* and *finally*.

Paraphrasing 1

Say, "You must choose your words carefully when you paraphrase. Listen as I read each sentence. Decide whether each statement is true or false. If a statement is false, change a word in the sentence so that it is true and say it to me."

(Note: Example sentences are provided for each false response.)

1. Something that is difficult is easy.
   (false; Something that is difficult is hard.)

2. A tame animal is easy to control. *(true)*

3. A delicious sandwich tastes bad.
   (false; A delicious sandwich tastes good.
   A stale sandwich tastes bad.)

4. You should believe someone who is telling the truth. *(true)*

5. You'll probably get excellent grades if you don't study.
   (false; You'll probably get poor grades if you don't study.
   You'll probably get excellent grades if you study.)

6. The best way to stay healthy is to eat junk food.
   (false; The best way to stay healthy is to eat healthy food.
   The worst way to stay healthy is to eat junk food.)

7. It's dangerous to play ball near a busy street. *(true)*

8. You should stay home from school if you are feeling fine.
   (false; You should stay home from school if you are feeling sick.
   You should go to school if you are feeling fine.)

9. Someone who is attractive is good looking. *(true)*

10. You should answer the telephone politely. *(true)*

11. Rules should always be ignored.
    (false; Rules should always be followed.
    Rules should never be ignored.)

12. A knife cuts better with a dull edge.
    (false; A knife cuts better with a sharp edge.)

Paraphrasing 2 ✓

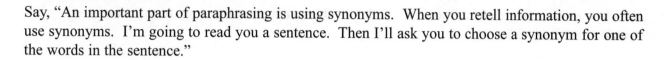

Say, "An important part of paraphrasing is using synonyms. When you retell information, you often use synonyms. I'm going to read you a sentence. Then I'll ask you to choose a synonym for one of the words in the sentence."

1. I have *searched* everywhere for my key.
   Which of these words could replace *searched*?   *(looked)*   lost

2. Please *deliver* this note to your mother.
   Which of these words could replace *deliver*?   remove   *(give)*

3. I *tugged* on the string as hard as I could.
   Which of these words could replace *tugged*?   pushed   *(pulled)*

4. She doesn't need any *extra* help.
   Which of these words could replace *extra*?   *(more)*   less

5. I'm *amazed* that he plays the piano.
   Which of these words could replace *amazed*?   *(shocked)*   done

6. We're *unhappy* because our dog is lost.
   Which of these words could replace *unhappy*?   *(sad)*   cheerful

7. We picked up *litter* along the road.
   Which of these words could replace *litter*?   treasure   *(trash)*

8. I hope you are over your *illness*.
   Which of these words could replace *illness*?   healthy   *(sickness)*

9. I think we had a very good *discussion*.
   Which of these words could replace *discussion*?   *(talk)*   activity

10. My brother *discovered* a great hot dog place.
    Which of these words could replace *discovered*?   *(found)*   avoided

Paraphrasing 3

Say, "I'm going to read you two sentences. Tell me if both sentences mean about the same thing or if they mean something different."

1. We are riding the bus to the zoo.
   We are taking the bus to the zoo. *(same)*

2. That box of crackers is almost empty.
   That box of crackers is almost full. *(different)*

3. My dad just bought a new computer.
   My dad just bought a used computer. *(different)*

4. Do you like playing baseball?
   Do you enjoy playing baseball? *(same)*

5. The fireplace was still blazing at midnight.
   The fireplace was still burning at midnight. *(same)*

6. The show got over later than we expected.
   The show got over earlier than we expected. *(different)*

7. The bread on the counter is the freshest.
   The bread on the counter is the newest. *(same)*

8. She was tired after her long trip.
   She was rested after her long trip. *(different)*

9. I require three things before I start the project.
   I need three things before I start the project. *(same)*

10. That bright computer screen is really hurting my eyes.
    That dim computer screen is really hurting my eyes. *(different)*

Paraphrasing 4

I'm going to read you two sentences. Tell me if both sentences mean about the same thing or if their meanings are different.

1. That CD is one of my mom's favorites.
   My mom really likes listening to that CD. *(same)*

2. I'm not familiar with the rules of that game.
   I can play that game very well. *(different)*

3. The baby won't cry if you hold her.
   Holding the baby keeps her happy. *(same)*

4. Could you hand me that hammer?
   Please give me that hammer. *(same)*

5. I'm a big fan of professional football.
   Professional football doesn't interest me. *(different)*

6. Where do you go to purchase clothes?
   Can you tell me where you buy your clothes? *(same)*

7. We enjoyed the way our teacher read the book.
   Our teacher didn't entertain us with her reading. *(different)*

8. It takes us a long time to drive to grandma's house.
   Our grandma doesn't live very far from us. *(different)*

9. The steak was so thick I couldn't eat it all.
   That huge steak was too much for me to eat. *(same)*

10. I thought the graphics on the video game were cool.
    That video game was really hard to play. *(different)*

Paraphrasing 5

Say, "I'll say a word. Then I'll use that word in a sentence. You repeat the sentence, but replace the word that I say with a synonym. For example, I say, '**sick** – I feel sick today.' A synonym for *sick* is *ill*, so you would answer, 'I feel ill today.'"

(Note: Examples of student answers are provided. Your students' word choices might vary.)

1. **simple** – That math test was simple. *(That math test was easy.)*

2. **brief** – We took a *brief* walk. *(We took a short walk.)*

3. **jog** – I like to jog in the mornings. *(I like to run in the mornings.)*

4. **ship** – The ship was over 200 hundred feet long. *(The boat was over 200 hundred feet long.)*

5. **upset** – I'm upset with the way you treated me. *(I'm angry with the way you spoke to me.)*

6. **speak** – Did you speak to him about your problem? *(Did you talk to him about your problem?)*

7. **chilly** – It is very chilly outside. *(It is very cold outside.)*

8. **complicated** – The directions are very complicated. *(The directions are very hard.)*

9. **frighten** – Roller coasters frighten my dad. *(Roller coasters scare my dad.)*

10. **illustrations** – Did you see the illustrations in that book? *(Did you see the drawings in that book?)*

11. **photographs** – I took a lot of photographs on vacation. *(I took a lot of pictures on vacation.)*

12. **lengthy** – I was tired after a lengthy day at school. *(I was tired after a long day at school.)*

Paraphrasing 6

Say, "I'll say a word. Then I'll use that word in a sentence. You repeat the sentence, but replace the word that I say with a synonym. For example, I say, '**huge** – That elephant was huge.' A synonym for *huge* is *enormous*, so you would answer, 'That elephant is enormous.'"

(Note: Examples of student answers are provided. Your students' word choices might vary.)

1. **concealing** – What are you concealing in your locker? (*What are you hiding in your locker?*)

2. **investigated** – The scientists investigated every corner of the huge cave. (*The scientists explored every corner of the huge cave.*)

3. **specific** – I gave her the most specific answer I possibly could. (*I gave her the most accurate answer I possibly could.*)

4. **exterminated** – The guy from Super Bug came and exterminated all of our cockroaches. (*The guy from Super Bug came and killed all of our cockroaches.*)

5. **partially** – I only partially agree with what you say. (*I only partly agree with what you say.*)

6. **peculiar** – That really was a peculiar thing to do in a public place. (*That really was a strange thing to do in a public place.*)

7. **hazardous** – It is hazardous to ride a bicycle without a helmet. (*It is dangerous to ride a bicycle without a helmet.*)

8. **perhaps** – Perhaps you could take out the garbage on your way to school. (*Maybe you could take out the garbage on your way to school.*)

9. **striking** – Are you going somewhere nice in that striking outfit? (*Are you going somewhere nice in that beautiful outfit?*)

10. **tangy** – I need a glass of water after eating that tangy sauce. (*I need a glass of water after eating that spicy sauce.*)

Paraphrasing 7

Say, "I'll say some words. Then I'll use those words in a sentence. You repeat the sentence, but replace the words that I say with synonyms. For example, I say, '**huge** and **ill** – That huge elephant is ill.' A synonym for *huge* is *enormous* and a synonym for *ill* is *sick*, so you would answer, 'That enormous elephant is sick.'"

(Note: Answers provided are examples only. Your students' word choices might vary.)

1. **consumed** and **tasty** – We consumed a tasty lunch. (*We ate a delicious lunch.*)

2. **viewed** and **rotten** – Last night we viewed a rotten movie. (*Last night we watched a bad movie.*)

3. **received** and **note** – I just received a note from someone at my old school. (*I just got a letter from someone at my old school.*)

4. **strolled** and **departed** – I strolled over to your house, but your mom said you had already departed. (*I walked over to your house, but your mom said you had already left.*)

5. **crispy** and **stale** – I like my chips nice and crispy. Those are stale. (*I like my chips nice and crunchy. Those are old.*)

6. **arguing, lengthy,** and **discussion** – My mom thought we were arguing, but we were just having a lengthy discussion. (*My mom thought we were fighting, but we were just having a long talk.*)

7. **toured, fascinating,** and **area** – Have you ever toured the state capitol? It's a fascinating area. (*Have you ever visited the state capitol? It's an interesting place.*)

8. **deliver, sketches,** and **instructor** – She asked me to deliver the sketches to her instructor. (*She asked me to take the drawings to her teacher.*)

Paraphrasing 8

Say, "When you say something in your own words, you have to get the basic information correct. Listen carefully to each of these instructions. Decide what is the single most important piece of information you need to remember. Then use as few words as possible to state the important information."

(Note: Answers provided are examples only. Your students' answers will vary.)

1. The bus will leave at exactly 8:00. If you aren't at the school at that time, you will be left behind. *(bus will leave at 8:00)*

2. That store is only open on weekdays. If you try to go there on Saturday or Sunday, it will be closed. *(only open on weekdays)*

3. If you don't follow my instructions, you could get very sick. Remember to take just one pill every morning. *(take one pill every morning)*

4. I'd be glad to let you use my computer. Just promise me that if something goes wrong, you won't try to fix it. *(don't try to fix anything that goes wrong)*

5. Listen carefully so you don't do more work than you need to. Open your math book to page 122. Do only the odd numbered problems for tomorrow. *(do only odd numbered problems on page 122)*

6. You can have ice cream after you finish your homework, not before. I think I bought your favorite flavor. You like chocolate, don't you? *(can have ice cream after homework)*

7. Make sure you bring $13 for the field trip. The money is for the bus and for lunch. If you don't bring money, you won't get to eat lunch. *(bring $13 for field trip)*

8. The last time someone borrowed my hair dryer they broke it. It's important that you turn it off before you unplug it. If you don't, it will blow a fuse and won't work. *(turn it off before you unplug it)*

9. I need you to run to the store for me. I need a one-liter bottle of corn oil. Make sure you get corn oil — not vegetable, sunflower, or canola oil. *(need a one-liter bottle of corn oil)*

10. I can't say this enough times. Don't ever copy any files onto my computer. You might have a virus on your disk. If it gets into my machine, I'll have big problems. *(don't copy files onto my computer)*

Paraphrasing 9

Say, "I'm going to read you some information about U.S. Presidents. I want you to tell me the information in one complete sentence using your own words. Focus on the most important information, and begin your sentence with the name of the President. Here's an example:

Andrew Jackson was one of the most interesting U.S. Presidents. He actually believed the Earth was flat. *(Andrew Jackson believed the earth was flat.)*"

(Note: Sample student answers are provided. Your students' answers may vary.)

1. John Tyler's White House was very crowded. He had 15 children. That's the most of any President. *(John Tyler had 15 children; John Tyler had more children than any President.)*

2. Abraham Lincoln is famous for many things. Did you know he was the first President to wear a beard in office? *(Abraham Lincoln was the first President to wear a beard.)*

3. Chester Arthur is known for his clothes. It is said he changed his pants several times a day. *(Chester Arthur changed his pants several times a day.)*

4. Teddy Roosevelt is known for a famous Presidential first. He took a short ride in an airplane. *(Teddy Roosevelt was the first President to ride in an airplane.)*

5. The President is on TV all the time today. Harry Truman was the first to appear on it. *(Harry Truman was the first President to be on TV.)*

6. Lyndon Johnson wasn't impressed by fancy food. One of his favorite things to eat was canned peas. *(Lyndon Johnson liked to eat canned peas.)*

7. Richard Nixon was known as quite a traveler. He visited all 50 states. *(Richard Nixon visited all 50 states.)*

8. Before Jimmy Carter, no other President had been born in a hospital. He was the first. *(Jimmy Carter was the first President born in a hospital.)*

9. Maybe Ronald Reagan didn't think a President would look good in glasses. He was the first to wear contact lenses. *(Ronald Reagan was the first President to wear contact lenses.)*

10. Bill Clinton had a strange experience when he was just eight years old. He was attacked by a sheep. *(Bill Clinton was attacked by a sheep when he was eight years old.)*

Paraphrasing 10

Say, "I'm going to read you some information about Africa. I want you to tell me the information in one complete sentence using your own words. Try to use as few words as possible while still telling the most important information. Here's an example:

> A larger number of people live in Africa than you might think. You'll find ten percent of the Earth's population lives there. *(Ten percent of the Earth's population lives in Africa.)*"

(Note: Sample student answers are provided. Your students' answers may vary.)

1. It would take you a long time to list all the countries in Africa. There are 50 of them all together. *(There are 50 countries in Africa; Africa is made up of 50 countries.)*

2. One-fourth of the land in Africa is taken up by a hot, dry area. That area is known as the Sahara Desert. *(The Sahara Desert makes up one-fourth of the land in Africa.)*

3. Asia is the largest continent in the world. It is the only continent larger than Africa. *(Africa is the second largest continent in the world; Asia is the only continent larger than Africa.)*

4. Many people think the Amazon is the world's longest river. In fact, the Nile River in Africa is longer. *(The Nile in Africa is the world's longest river.)*

5. African lions aren't always hunting and running around. In fact, most of them sleep twenty hours a day. *(African lions sleep twenty hours a day.)*

6. There are many chimpanzees in Africa, and they like to hang out together. They can live in groups of a hundred or more. *(Chimpanzees can live in groups of a hundred or more.)*

7. Victoria Falls is a spectacular site in Africa. The famous waterfall is over a hundred meters high. That's longer than the length of a football field. *(Victoria Falls is one hundred meters high; Victoria Falls is longer than a football field.)*

8. You can still see the animals Africa is most famous for. There are many national parks in Africa where the animals are kept and protected. *(You can see African animals in national parks.)*

Paraphrasing 11

Say, "I'm going to read you some information about the weather. I want you to tell me the information in one complete sentence using your own words. Try to use as few words as possible while still telling the most important information. Here's an example:

> Have you ever noticed that it's cooler in the country than it is in the city? That's because city buildings, streets, and concrete trap the heat from the Sun. *(It's warmer in the city than it is in the country because cities trap heat.)*"

(Note: Sample student answers are provided. Your students' answers may vary.)

1. Some animals decide to take a sort of vacation during the cold winter months. They hibernate, or go to sleep for a few months and wake up in the spring. *(Some animals hibernate in the winter and wake up in the spring.)*

2. No two snowflakes are ever the same. The one thing they all have in common is that each snowflake has six points. Other than that, each snowflake looks different. *(Snowflakes have six points, but they all look different.)*

3. Tornadoes are one of nature's most destructive forces. The U.S. has about 700 of them every year. Luckily, few of them do any serious damage. *(The U.S. has about 700 tornadoes every year, but few do any serious damage.)*

4. Why did the dinosaurs disappear? Could it have been because the Earth became too cold for them to survive? Some scientists think so. *(Some scientists think the dinosaurs disappeared because the Earth became too cold for them.)*

5. Do you like it hot? Maybe you should move to Death Valley, California. A temperature of 134 degrees was once measured there. That's the highest of any place in the United States. *(The highest temperature ever in the United States was 134 degrees at Death Valley, California.)*

6. Most people think of India as a very dry country. You'll be interested to know that for one year a town in India was the wettest in the world. It received over 1,000 inches of rain. *(The most rain to fall in a year was over 1,000 inches on a town in India.)*

7. There's a place in Chile where you won't find much green grass. Not a drop of rain was measured there in one fourteen-year period. *(No rain fell in a place in Chile for fourteen years.)*

Discerning Important Information

100% Listening – Intermediate

Paraphrasing 12

Say, "I'm going to read you some information. Listen carefully and remember the most important things I say. Then tell me the information in your own words."

(Note: Answers will vary.)

1. Have you ever thought about what goes into the fast food you order? To start with, the meat might have come from a cattle ranch in Montana. The wheat for the bun could have been grown in Kansas. The lettuce and tomato were probably grown in California. All these items are brought together into one sandwich you can hold in your hand.

2. The fast-food French fry is an amazing thing. You might not believe it but a lot of technology goes into one order of fries. Specially grown potatoes are sorted and peeled by robotic machines. Then they are shot with a high pressure water cannon through a slicer. Each fry is cut to the exact same size. Scanners and computers then sort them again. Any fry that is discolored or the wrong shape is blown off the line by a puff of air. The fries are then often injected with flavorings, including beef flavor. That's what gives them that special taste. The last step is to fry them in oil that is the perfect temperature.

3. Are you always getting exactly what you expect at a fast-food restaurant? Did you know that potatoes aren't only used for French fries anymore? Many times the bun for your hamburger was made using potato flour. And that might not exactly be a milk shake you're drinking. Some fast-food shakes are actually made with specially-prepared and flavored potatoes.

Paraphrasing 13

Say, "I'm going to read you some assignments. When I'm finished, I want you to give me the steps you'll need to take to complete each assignment. It might help if you use words like *first, next, after that,* and *finally*."

(Note: Answers will vary.)

Assignment 1

Since we are talking about immigration in social studies, I'd like each of you to complete a family tree. The assignment will be due one week from today. Begin by asking your mom or dad to help you list all the people in your family. Find out the names and ages of grandparents, aunts, uncles, and cousins. I will give you a special form to keep track of the names. Then you can present your information in any way you'd like.

Assignment 2

Instead of a test at the end of this math unit, we are going to try something different. I would like you to start by forming teams of three. I won't assign you to a team. You will have to form your own teams. Since we have been studying measurement, each team will do a measuring project. Your team will choose a building to measure. I want you to find the total area and volume of the building. Make sure your answers are in metric measurements.

Assignment 3

There are two things I'd like to get done after lunch today. The more important of those two is to finish your science experiment. Let's get that started right after you get in the classroom. You don't even have to wait for me to tell you to begin. Just get your things together and go to it. The other thing we need to do is choose a topic for our social studies project. I hope you've been thinking about that. If we get that done and have some time left over, you can work on your book report. Have a good lunch.

Paraphrasing 14

Say, "I'm going to read you some directions for getting someplace or doing something. When I'm finished, I want you to give me the steps you'll need to take to complete each assignment. It might help if you use words like *first, next, after that,* and *finally*."

(Note: Answers will vary.)

Making a Great Hamburger

Everyone likes something different on a hamburger. Here's the way I think it should be done. First of all, cook your hamburger all the way through. It should be well-done with no pink on the inside. Toast a whole wheat bun on the grill. Top your burger with a thin tomato slice, brown mustard, and steak sauce. If you really want to make it great, add some grilled onions.

Getting to the Airport

Driving to the airport is a real pain. I think I have the best way to get there. Take a bus or taxi to the downtown train station. Take the Blue Line Airport Express train. Make sure you take the express because it doesn't make any stops. When you get to the airport, don't go in through the front entrance. That's the big mistake everyone makes. Go down the outside stairs and use the lower level entrance. It's always much less crowded.

Going on a Bicycle Trip

A bicycle trip will be a lot more fun if you take some time to prepare. The first thing you need to consider is safety. Always wear a helmet. Also, a spare tire tube and small air pump are essential. If you pack food or extra clothes, be careful. The weight of these things can add up. A loaded backpack or bike bag will change the way you ride. Take a fully-loaded trial run before you leave on your trip. The most important thing to remember is not to take anything that you don't need.

Identifying Details

Listening is a skill that's practiced to a great extent in the classroom. In fact, your students spend over half of their school day listening to directions, explanations, announcements, and much more. When your students listen to any type of message, they need to be able to distinguish the important details. If your students don't know how to listen for these details, they will have trouble understanding the message.

To better understand a message, students must ask questions about what they are hearing. Who is the message about? Where is the activity going to be? When do I need to be there? What do I need to bring with me? Why do I need to go? How much will the activity cost? If the students can answer these types of questions, they can pinpoint the important details of the message.

In this unit, your students will focus on the *who, what, where, when, why,* and *how* of information. They will work on:

- answering *wh-* and *how* questions about sentences
- identifying pronoun referents
- differentiating facts from opinions
- answering *wh-* and *how* questions about math problems
- answering *wh-* and *how* questions about advertisements
- answering *wh-* and *how* questions about short stories

Present the stimuli at a normal speaking rate. If a student has trouble answering, slow your presentation rate.

Identifying Details 1

Who Questions

Say, "Listen carefully. Then answer my question."

1. Thomas Edison invented the light bulb. Who invented the light bulb? *(Thomas Edison)*

2. An author is a person who writes a book or story. Who is an author? *(person who writes a book or story)*

3. A baby-sitter takes care of children when their parents are at work or away from home. Who takes care of children when their parents are at work or away from home? *(baby-sitter)*

4. A chauffeur is a person who is hired to drive a car or a limousine. Who is a chauffeur? *(person hired to drive a car or limousine)*

5. A passenger is a person who travels in a vehicle. She does not drive the vehicle she rides in. Who travels in a vehicle but does not drive it? *(passenger)*

6. A tenant pays rent to live in a house or an apartment. Who pays rent to live in a house or an apartment? *(tenant)*

What Questions

Say, "Listen carefully. Then answer my question."

1. The stomach is a body organ that stores and digests food. What is a body organ that stores and digests food? *(stomach)*

2. J. K. Rowling is a well-known English author. She wrote the popular Harry Potter books. What did J. K. Rowling write? *(Harry Potter books)*

3. A tornado is a funnel-shaped cloud that spins very fast. It is also known as a twister. What is another name for a tornado? *(twister)*

4. When you add two numbers together, you get the sum of those numbers. What is the sum of eleven and nine? *(twenty)*

5. A meteorologist is a scientist who studies the Earth's atmosphere and predicts the weather. What does a meteorologist do? *(studies Earth's atmosphere, predicts the weather)*

6. Timber is wood that will be used to build things like houses and boats. What is timber used for? *(to build things like houses and boats)*

Identifying Details 2

Where Questions

Say, "Listen carefully. Then answer my question."

1. Ontario is a province in Canada. Where is Ontario? *(Canada)*

2. Koalas and kangaroos are two animals that live in Australia. Where do koalas and kangaroos live? *(Australia)*

3. Periscopes are used in submarines to see above the surface of the water. Where would you find a periscope? *(submarine)*

4. Raccoons, deer, and squirrels are some of the many animals that live in a forest. Where do deer live? *(forest)*

5. Chicago is a large city in Illinois. It sits on the shore of Lake Michigan. Where is Chicago? *(Illinois, on shore of Lake Michigan)*

6. A piece of land where fruit trees are grown is called an orchard. Where would you find fruit trees growing? *(orchard)*

When Questions

Say, "Listen carefully. Then answer my question."

1. Dr. James Naismith invented the game of basketball in 1891. When was basketball invented? *(1891)*

2. You make an appointment to see your doctor when you are not feeling well. When do you make an appointment with your doctor? *(when you're not feeling well)*

3. Some animals hibernate, or sleep, all winter long. When do some animals hibernate? *(winter)*

4. Many students attend a college or a university after they graduate from high school. When do students attend a college or a university? *(after they graduate from high school)*

5. After you mix the eggs and sugar together, add a cup of flour. When do you add a cup of flour? *(after you mix the eggs and sugar together)*

6. In football, you kick an extra point after your team scores a touchdown. When do you kick an extra point in football? *(after your team scores a touchdown)*

Identifying Details 3

Why Questions

Say, "Listen carefully. Then answer my question."

1. The words *late* and *early* are antonyms because they have opposite meanings. Why are the words *late* and *early* antonyms? *(They have opposite meanings.)*

2. Never stand under a tree when it's lightning because lightning often strikes the tallest object on the ground. Why shouldn't you stand under a tree when it's lightning? *(Lightning often strikes the tallest object on the ground.)*

3. Ambulances have sirens to warn people to get out of their way. Why do ambulances have sirens? *(to warn people to get out of their way)*

4. People take vitamins to help keep their bodies healthy. Why do people take vitamins? *(to keep their bodies healthy)*

5. People take vacations to relax and enjoy time with their families. Why do people take vacations? *(to relax and enjoy time with their families)*

6. You should be quiet in a library so you don't disturb other people who are reading or studying. Why should you be quiet in a library? *(so you don't disturb other people)*

How Questions

Say, "Listen carefully. Then answer my question."

1. There are 100 years in a century. How many years are in a century? *(100)*

2. A millionaire is a person who has at least a million dollars. How much money does a millionaire have? *(million dollars or more)*

3. You can determine how old a tree is by counting its tree rings. How can you figure out how old a tree is? *(by counting its tree rings)*

4. A diver uses a scuba tank to breathe underwater. How does a diver breathe underwater? *(uses a scuba tank)*

5. February usually has 28 days, but in a leap year it has 29 days. How many days does February have in a leap year? *(29)*

6. A vaccine protects a person by making him immune to a disease. How does a vaccine protect someone? *(makes him immune to a disease)*

Identifying Details 4

Say, "Listen carefully. Then answer my question."

1. A fugitive is a person who is running away from the police. Who is a fugitive? *(person who is running away from the police)*

2. You frown when you are unhappy. When do you frown? *(when you are unhappy)*

3. Spanish moss is an unusual plant because it has no roots. Why is Spanish moss an unusual plant? *(has no roots)*

4. A biography is the story of a person's life written by another person. What is a biography? *(story of a person's life written by another person)*

5. A person who writes the story of his own life is writing an autobiography. Who writes an autobiography? *(person who writes the story of his own life)*

6. The cockpit is the part of the airplane where the pilot sits. Where does a pilot sit in an airplane? *(cockpit)*

7. The Heimlich maneuver is an emergency treatment that is used when someone is choking. When is the Heimlich maneuver used? *(when someone is choking)*

8. A medical illustrator is a person who draws diagrams of the human body. Who is a medical illustrator? *(person who draws diagrams of the human body)*

9. Confetti is tiny pieces of colored paper that people throw in the air. What is confetti? *(tiny pieces of colored paper that people throw in the air)*

10. You should have a dental checkup every six months. How often should you have a dental checkup? *(every six months)*

11. Many people get homesick when they have been away from home too long. When do people get homesick? *(when they've been away from home too long)*

12. An arena is an enclosed space where sporting events and concerts can be held. Where can sporting events and concerts be held? *(arena)*

13. There are 206 bones in the human body. How many bones do you have in your body? *(206)*

14. On Veteran's Day, we honor the men and women who have served in the armed forces. When do we honor the men and women who have served in the armed forces? *(Veteran's Day)*

15. During an eclipse of the Sun, the Sun is hidden because the moon is passing between the Sun and the Earth. Why is the Sun hidden during an eclipse? *(because the moon is passing between the Sun and the Earth)*

Identifying Details 5

Say, "Listen carefully. Then answer my question."

1. A hobby is something a person likes to do in his spare time. What is a hobby? *(something a person likes to do in his spare time)*

2. A hero is someone you look up to. Who is a hero? *(someone you look up to)*

3. A person who is not willing to work or try hard might be considered lazy. Why would someone be considered lazy? *(not willing to work or try hard)*

4. If you wanted to climb to the top of the Eiffel Tower, you would have to climb 1,710 steps. How many steps do you need to climb to get to the top of the Eiffel Tower? *(1,710)*

5. An anchor is a heavy object that is dropped into the water to keep a boat from drifting. Why would you drop an anchor into the water? *(to keep a boat from drifting)*

6. If you visit London, England, you would see Big Ben and Buckingham Palace. Where would you go to see Buckingham Palace? *(London, England)*

7. A narrator is a person who tells a story. Who is a narrator? *(person who tells a story)*

8. A messenger carries messages or runs errands. What does a messenger do? *(carries messages or runs errands)*

9. Water freezes at 32 degrees Fahrenheit and boils at 212 degrees Fahrenheit. When does water boil? *(212 degrees Fahrenheit)*

10. A vault is a room in a bank where money and other valuables are kept. Where would you see a vault? *(bank)*

11. Homes and businesses need addresses to receive mail and so that people can find where you live or work. Why do homes and businesses need addresses? *(to receive mail and so that people can find where you live or work)*

12. Florida, California, and Texas are all famous for their orange groves. What is one state that is famous for orange groves? *(Florida, California, Texas)*

13. Many people put advertisements in the newspaper because they want to sell something. Why do people put advertisements in the newspaper? *(because they want to sell something)*

14. You can find out what's happening in the world by watching the news every evening. How can you find out what's happening the world? *(watch the news every evening)*

15. Someone who wants to remember the things she does or the things she thinks about each day might write everything down in a diary. Why would someone write in a diary? *(to remember things she did and the things she thinks about)*

Identifying Details 6

Say, "Listen carefully to each sentence. Then tell me who or what the pronoun refers to."

1. A compass rose is found on a map. *It* shows you the four main directions – north, south, east, and west. What is *it*? *(compass rose)*

2. Oceans are large bodies of salt water. *They* cover over half of the Earth's surface. What are *they*? *(oceans)*

3. Soil conservation is very important to farmers. *They* know *they* must have rich topsoil to grow food. That is why *they* have learned different ways to protect the topsoil. Who are *they*? *(farmers)*

4. Sometimes farmers plant rows of trees along the sides of their fields. These trees slow down the wind so *it* doesn't blow the topsoil away. What is *it*? *(wind)*

5. Computers have become a very important part of our lives. Most businesses would not be able to operate without *them*. What are *them*? *(computers)*

6. A cowboy is a man who works on a ranch. *He* takes care of the cattle. Who is *he*? *(cowboy)*

7. Pioneer families traveled west on the Oregon Trail. Most of *them* were heading West to claim land for their homes and farms. Who are *them*? *(pioneer families)*

8. John Chapman lived in the late 1700s. Many people called *him* Johnny Appleseed because he planted apple trees everywhere he went. Who is *him*? *(John Chapman)*

9. When Samantha Smith was just eleven years old, *she* sent a letter to the leader of the Soviet Union. Samantha told the leader *she* was frightened of nuclear war. Who is *she*? *(Samantha Smith)*

10. When the leader of the Soviet Union received Samantha's letter, he invited *her* to visit the Soviet Union. Who is *her*? *(Samantha Smith)*

11. Bayou is an odd-sounding word. *It* is a stream that moves slowly through a swampy area. What is *it*? *(bayou)*

12. My grandmother and I took a trip to Egypt. While *we* were there, *we* went to see the pyramids. Who are *we*? *(my grandmother and I)*

13. Robert said, "*I* am going to make a donation to the Red Cross. It's an organization that helps a lot of people!" Who is *I*? *(Robert)*

14. I am a descendent of Matthew Thornton. *He* was one of the men who signed the Declaration of Independence. Who is *he*? *(Matthew Thornton)*

Identifying Details 7

Say, "Listen carefully to each sentence. Then tell me who or what the pronoun refers to."

1. The St. Lawrence Seaway is an important waterway. *It* connects Lake Ontario to the Atlantic Ocean. What is *it*? *(St. Lawrence Seaway)*

2. My sister doesn't feel well today. My dad stayed home from work so he could take *her* to the doctor. Who is *her*? *(my sister)*

3. Roadrunners are birds that live in the desert. *They* are unusual birds. Most of the time *they* run instead of fly. What are *they*? *(roadrunners)*

4. Frank Lloyd Wright was a famous architect. *He* designed many different buildings and houses. Who is *he*? *(Frank Lloyd Wright)*

5. Many people live on river banks. Some of these people protect their homes from flooding by building *them* up on stilts. What are *them*? *(homes)*

6. We had a big snowstorm during the night. When Carter and I woke up, our mom told *us* school was cancelled for the day. Who are *us*? *(Carter and I)*

7. Your teacher told you to draw an octagon. You drew a shape with six sides. When your teacher saw your drawing, *she* said, "That's wrong. An octagon has eight sides." Who is *she*? *(teacher)*

8. The Statue of Liberty is a symbol of freedom. *She* holds her torch high to tell everyone that the United States is a free country. Who is *she*? *(Statue of Liberty)*

9. Hogans are mound-like buildings made from mud and logs. The mud walls keep *them* cool in the summer and warm in the winter. What are *them*? *(hogans)*

10. Bats are the only mammals that can really fly. The smallest bat is the bumblebee bat. *It* is about the size of a penny. What is *it*? *(bumblebee bat)*

11. Geysers are hot springs that shoot boiling water and steam high into the air. You can see many of *them* in Yellowstone National Park. What are *them*? *(geysers)*

12. My little brother asked me what the word "timid" means. I told *him* it means "shy." Who is *him*? *(little brother)*

13. July 20, 1969, was a monumental day for Astronaut Neil Armstrong. It was the day *he* became the first man to walk on the moon. Who is *he*? *(Neil Armstrong)*

14. An atlas is a book of maps. You use *it* to find out information about places all over the world. What is *it*? *(atlas)*

15. I helped my older sister collect food for the Student Hunger Drive. *We* asked our friends and neighbors to donate cans of food. Who are *we*? *(my older sister and I)*

Identifying Details 8

Say, "Listen carefully to each sentence. Then tell me if it is a fact or an opinion."

1. A triangle has three sides. *(fact)*

2. My brother is the most annoying person I know. *(opinion)*

3. On October 8, 1871, a terrible fire destroyed Chicago. *(fact)*

4. Pollution makes the air or water dirty and unhealthy. *(fact)*

5. American astronauts landed on the moon in 1969. *(fact)*

6. That song is the worst song I've ever heard! *(opinion)*

7. Autumn is the most beautiful time of the year. *(opinion)*

8. Dinosaurs have been extinct for millions of years. *(fact)*

9. Tokyo is the capital of Japan. *(fact)*

10. I don't think people should have to work on the weekend. *(opinion)*

11. The World Wide Web is a tool that helps people use the Internet. *(fact)*

12. I think the Internet is the best place to go to find information. *(opinion)*

13. You can always find a good bargain at Wally's Furniture World. *(opinion)*

14. My mom makes the best pizza in the world! *(opinion)*

15. If you are bilingual, you can speak two languages. *(fact)*

16. Abraham Lincoln was 6 feet, 4 inches tall, making him the tallest President of the United States. *(fact)*

17. Most people would rather go to a movie than stay home and watch TV. *(opinion)*

18. The Red Cross helps people who have been affected by war or natural disasters. *(fact)*

19. The fertile soil in the Midwest makes it the best area for growing many different crops. *(opinion)*

20. There are 24 time zones in the world, one for each hour of the day. *(fact)*

21. Earth is the third planet from the Sun. *(fact)*

22. The Great Wall of China is the only man-made object visible from the moon. *(fact)*

23. The best way to travel is by plane. *(opinion)*

24. "The Star Spangled Banner" is the United States' national anthem. *(fact)*

25. The thirteen stripes on the American flag stand for the thirteen original colonies. *(fact)*

Identifying Details 9

Say, "Listen carefully to these problems. Then answer the questions."

1. Are three, four, and six all even numbers? *(no)*

2. Is 79 more or less than 97? *(less)*

3. Is 101 greater than or less than 99? *(greater)*

4. Is nine plus nine equal to 18? *(yes)*

5. A very fast swimmer could swim 150 yards in a minute. Dolphins can swim 600 yards in a minute. Who swims faster – a dolphin or a man? *(dolphin)*

6. The Empire State Building is 1,250 feet tall. The Sears Tower is 1,453 feet tall. Which building is taller? *(Sears Tower)*

7. Emily and Molly each bought a new book. Emily paid $12 for her book. Molly paid $10 for hers. Who paid more for her book? *(Emily)*

8. There are six empty juice boxes. You drank three of them. Did you drink half of them? *(yes)*

9. A yard is equal to three feet. If a football field is 100 yards long, how many feet long is it? *(300)*

10. Four boys are going to share a pizza. The pizza is cut into 12 pieces. How many pieces of pizza should each boy get? *(three)*

11. Ms. Gonzales has 62 papers to grade. She has already graded half of them. How many more papers does Ms. Gonzales have to grade before she is finished? *(31, the other half)*

12. Heather got five cards for her birthday. Each card had $10 in it. How much money did Heather get for her birthday? *($50)*

13. A new baseball glove costs $65. If someone paid for the glove with a $100 bill, how much change would the person get back? *($35)*

14. A person weighs six times as much on the Earth as he does on the moon. If you weigh ten pounds on the moon, how much will you weigh on the Earth? *(60 pounds)*

15. There are eight pints in a gallon. There are two cups in each pint. How many cups are in a gallon? *(16)*

16. Seth has two dozen cookies. He wants to give one cookie to each child in his class. There are 27 children in Seth's class. Does Seth have enough cookies? *(no)* How many more cookies does he need? *(three)*

Identifying Details 10

Say, "Listen carefully to these advertisements. Then answer the questions."

1. For Sale: white refrigerator, five years old, excellent condition, $350. Call 942-6621.
   What color is the refrigerator? *(white)*
   How old is it? *(five years)*

2. Baby-sitter needed for two children, ages three and five. Must be available Mondays through Fridays from 8 a.m. to 5 p.m. Will pay $5.00 an hour. Call 224-2287.
   What job is this ad for? *(baby-sitter)*
   How much will the baby-sitter be paid? *($5.00 an hour)*

3. Wanted: Home for pot-bellied pig. Makes a great pet. Loves children. Free to good home. Call 673-7762.
   What needs a good home? *(pot-bellied pig)*
   How much is the pig? *(It's free.)*

4. Home For Sale by Owner: Three-bedrooms; two baths; located on a quiet, dead-end street. $75,000. Call 853-3233 for more information.
   Who is selling this home? *(the owner)*
   Where is the house located? *(quiet, dead-end street)*

5. For Sale: Two tickets to the Chicago Bears/Green Bay Packers football game on October 14th. Tickets are $45 each. Call 743-2658.
   What is for sale? *(two football tickets)*
   When is the game? *(October 14th)*
   How much is each ticket? *($45)*

Say, "Some important information is missing from each of these advertisements. Listen carefully to each ad. Then answer the question."

1. Garage Sale: Saturday from 9 a.m. to 3 p.m.
   What else do you need to know if you want to go to this garage sale? *(address)*

2. Job Opening: Waitress needed at Dave's Diner. No experience necessary. Call to make an appointment for an interview.
   What else do you need to know if you want to apply for this job? *(phone number)*

3. Lost dog. If you find my dog, please call 842-1123.
   What else do you need to know if you want to help this person find her dog? *(what dog looks like)*

4. Don't miss our grand opening! Spencer's Sports Store, 1919 53rd Ave., Springfield, IL.
   What else do you need to know if you want to go to this grand opening? *(when it is)*

Identifying Details 11

Say, "Listen carefully while I tell you a story. Then I'll ask questions to see how well you listened."

1. Do you know what a flea market is? It sounds like a place where you go to buy fleas, but it's not. It's a market where people set up stands and sell old or used items.

   What is a flea market? *(market where people set up stands and sell old or used items)*

2. Stay away from windows during a hurricane. The wind from a hurricane can blow out the windows. The flying glass could injure you.

   Why should you stay away from windows during a hurricane? *(windows could break and the flying glass could injure you)*

3. The Tour de France is a 23-day bike race in France. People from all over the world come to participate in this race.

   What is the Tour de France? *(bike race)*
   How long is the race? *(23 days)*

4. When a mother crocodile senses danger, she keeps her babies safe by holding them in her mouth. Then, when the danger is over, she spits them out.

   How does a mother crocodile keep her babies safe from danger? *(holds them in her mouth)*
   What does she do when the danger is over? *(spits them out)*

5. A blind person reads by using Braille. Braille is made up of patterns of tiny raised bumps on paper. Each pattern represents a letter of the alphabet. The reader runs his fingers over the bumps and feels the letter patterns.

   Who uses Braille? *(blind people)*
   How does the person read Braille? *(runs his fingers over the bumps and feels the letter patterns)*

6. A meteor is another name for a falling star. Most meteors never fall to Earth. They burn up in the Earth's atmosphere before they reach the ground. However, sometimes meteors do fall to Earth. We call the material that lands on the Earth a meteorite.

   What is another name for a falling star? *(meteor)*
   What happens to most meteors? *(burn up in Earth's atmosphere)*
   What do we call a meteor that lands on the Earth? *(meteorite)*

7. If you like to hike, you might want to spend some time on the Appalachian National Scenic Trail. This trail is the longest marked footpath in the United States. It is 2,158 miles long and runs from Maine to Georgia. The footpath passes through 14 states. You can find your way along the path by following wooden signposts and white markings painted on rocks and trees.

   What is the Appalachian National Scenic Trail? *(longest marked footpath in the United States)*
   How many states does the trail pass through? *(14)*
   How can you find your way along the path? *(follow wooden signposts and white markings on rocks and trees)*

Main Idea

Determining the main idea of information your students hear allows them to extend conversations by making relevant remarks. In this section, your students will practice identifying and naming both main ideas and details. Near the end of the section, they will also explore the difference between topics and main ideas. This diagram might help your students understand how all the elements work together.

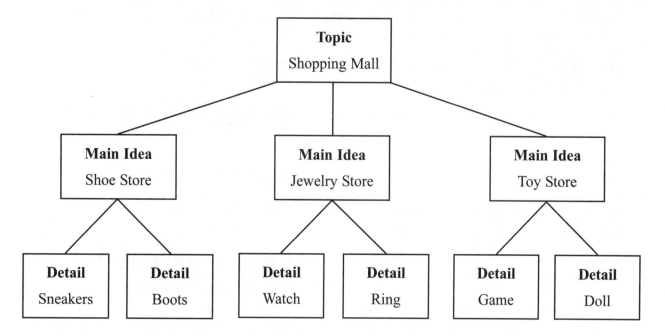

As your students work with main idea, encourage them to keep these factors in mind:

1. A topic is an overall theme for what is happening. Think of a topic as a shopping mall.

2. The main idea is what the information is about. Identifying main idea is a way of expressing what is going on. If a topic is a shopping mall, the main idea is an individual store in a mall.

3. Details support the main idea. They are sentences that support, or tell more about, the main idea. Think of details as the items sold in the store (main idea) inside the mall (topic).

Main Idea 1

Fold this page in half lengthwise so your student can only see the pictures as you read the main idea sentences.

Say, "Look at each picture. I'm going to read you three sentences for each picture. You tell me which sentence best expresses the main idea. Remember, the main idea is a short sentence that describes exactly what is happening. Use only the information from the picture to make your decision."

a. It is a beautiful morning.
b. *(The hot air balloons are taking off.)*
c. None of the balloons has crashed.

a. This concert just started.
b. This band is really good.
c. *(The singer is performing for his fans.)*

a. It is a close football game.
b. She can only kick this high once a game.
c. *(The cheerleader is excited about the game.)*

a. *(A person is looking at a painting.)*
b. The museum is about to close.
c. This is a popular painting at the museum.

Identifying Main Idea from Photograph
100% Listening – Intermediate

Main Idea 2

Say, "Listen as I read each paragraph. Then choose the sentence that best expresses the main idea."

1. Over 10,000 people jammed into the Arena last night. They were there to see one of today's most popular groups B4-All. It was the first sellout in the Arena's history.

   a. The B4-All concert was a great show.
   b. *(A sellout crowd saw the group B4-All.)*
   c. The Arena holds 10,000 people.

2. A dictionary is an important tool. It can help you in many ways. A dictionary can help you find out how to spell a word. It can also give you the word's definition. If you don't know how to pronounce a word, a dictionary can help.

   a. A dictionary can help you spell a word.
   b. You should keep a dictionary in your desk.
   c. *(A dictionary gives you a lot of information about a word.)*

3. What is the smallest city to have an NFL team? Only about 100,000 people live in Green Bay, Wisconsin. This small city is home to the Packers. The Packers are one of the oldest teams in the NFL. Even though the city is small, every game is sold out. Green Bay is very proud of its Packers.

   a. *(Green Bay is the smallest city with an NFL team.)*
   b. The Green Bay Packers are one of the best teams in the NFL.
   c. It is hard to get a ticket to a Packers game.

4. Computer skills are very important today. Almost every job uses a computer in some way. Even farmers rely on computers. If you want to be successful you need to get computer skills. You should know how to type. You should also know how to use the most common computer programs.

   a. Farmers spend a lot of time using computers.
   b. You can't get a job if you can't use a computer.
   c. *(Having computer skills might help you get a job.)*

Main Idea 3

Say, "Listen as I read each paragraph. Tell me a sentence that expresses the main idea."

1. Killer whales are beautiful. They are also the most dangerous of all whales. They eat almost anything in the ocean. Killer whales are about 30 feet long. They have long, sharp teeth. The whales hunt in groups, and they are very good at it. Seals are one of their favorite victims.

   (Killer whales are the most dangerous of all whales, Killer whales hunt and eat almost anything in the ocean.)

2. What do you think of when you hear the word *rattlesnake*? You probably think of words like *poisonous*, *bite*, and *attack*. You probably didn't say *gentle* or *quiet*. In fact, the rattlesnake is a gentle, easygoing snake. It would rather soak up the sun than strike your leg. If you frighten this quiet reptile, though, it will protect itself. Leave a rattlesnake alone, and it will continue to take it easy.

   (Rattlesnakes are normally gentle animals.)

3. The mammoth was a relative of today's elephants. Even though the two look alike, there are a few differences. First of all, the mammoth had a much larger head. It also had huge, curved tusks. Some mammoth tusks were so long, they crossed each other. Finally, the mammoth had long brown or red hair covering its body.

   (There are some differences between a mammoth and an elephant.)

4. Some kinds of turtles live on the water or on land and water. A tortoise is a type of turtle that lives only on land. Most tortoises move very slowly. They have large, dome-topped shells. The Galapagos tortoise is one of the largest turtles. It can weigh as much as 600 pounds.

   (facts about tortoises)

Main Idea 4

Say, "Supporting details are sentences or phrases that tell you more about a main idea. Listen for supporting details as I read you a paragraph. When I'm finished, I'll read you three phrases. You tell me if each one is a main idea or a supporting detail."

1. TV sitcoms seem to be getting worse. Twenty years ago, network sitcoms were funny and appropriate for the whole family. Today, the language and situations on sitcoms are only fit for adults. The shows aren't even funny. Only one or two new sitcoms even stay on TV for more than a year. People are turning off network sitcoms and watching cable shows instead.

    a. One or two new sitcoms stay on TV for more than a year. (*supporting detail*)
    b. TV sitcoms aren't as good today as they were in the past. (*main idea*)
    c. Language and situations are only fit for adults. (*supporting detail*)

2. Water makes up two-thirds of our bodies. That's why doctors tell us to drink lots of water. We should be drinking eight glasses of water every day. Fresh water makes our bodies healthier. It helps nutrients move through our bodies. It also helps regulate body temperature. Water is the most important part of our bodies.

    a. Drinking more water makes our bodies healthier. (*main idea*)
    b. Water helps nutrients move through our bodies. (*supporting detail*)
    c. We should drink eight glasses of water every day. (*supporting detail*)

3. Learning to play a musical instrument is difficult. It's also something you can do to make yourself smarter and happier. A musical instrument can do a lot for you. It can help you relax. That can reduce stress. Practicing helps you learn to focus and concentrate. Those are skills that you also need in your school work. Many kids who begin taking music lessons soon see their grades improve. Learning an instrument isn't just about making music. It's also about living a better life.

    a. Learning a musical instrument can help you relax and reduce stress. (*supporting detail*)
    b. Practicing an instrument helps you learn to focus and concentrate. (*supporting detail*)
    c. Learning a musical instrument can have an impact on your life. (*main idea*)

Main Idea 5

Say, "I'm going to read you a main idea and three details. You tell me which detail does not support the main idea."

1. Main Idea: The ocean is a great place for a vacation.

    a. There's something for everyone in the family to do at the ocean.
    b. *(You can eat at a restaurant.)*
    c. You can swim or just relax on the beach.

2. Main Idea: Computers are important to the automobile industry.

    a. *(Some computers break down a lot.)*
    b. Mechanics use computers to fix cars.
    c. New cars have computers in their engines.

3. Main Idea: Bicycle injuries can be prevented.

    a. Don't ride your bicycle on the sidewalk.
    b. Wear a helmet whenever you ride your bicycle.
    c. *(Riding a bicycle uphill takes a lot of energy.)*

4. Main Idea: Hockey goalie might be the most difficult position in sports.

    a. The puck comes at you at over 100 miles per hour.
    b. *(What do you think is the easiest position in sports?)*
    c. It's difficult to see through all the equipment you wear.

5. Main Idea: Telephones have changed a lot over the years.

    a. *(Almost every home has a phone.)*
    b. The first telephones didn't even have buttons.
    c. Some phones today let you send E-mail.

6. Main Idea: Some people would never live in a small town.

    a. There just isn't enough excitement in a small town.
    b. *(A small town is a good place to raise a family.)*
    c. Everyone in a small town knows too much about everyone else.

Main Idea 6

Say, "Listen carefully as I read each main idea and paragraph. Tell me which detail does not support the main idea."

1. Main Idea: How to become a good cook

   Almost anyone can cook. Few people can cook well. There are several ways you can become a good cook. One way is to cook alongside someone who is skilled. *(This also works with driving.)* Another way is to take cooking classes. Finally, you can watch cooking shows on TV. If you do any of those, you will soon be a good cook.

2. Main Idea: Keeping your heart healthy through exercise

   One way to live a long life is to keep your heart in shape. The best way to do that is through exercise. It doesn't take a ton of exercise to keep your heart healthy. Most people say that 20 minutes of exercise three times a week is all you need. *(You should also eat healthy foods.)* Just a small amount of exercise can make a big difference to your heart.

3. Main Idea: Color can affect your mood.

   Did you know that the color of a room can affect your mood? Many experiments show that color can influence how you feel. For example, darker colors like deep red and purple might make you anxious or uneasy. *(Red is not a favorite color of mine.)* Colors like light blue and green have a calming effect.

4. Main Idea: Libraries are still necessary.

   Computers were supposed to replace libraries long ago. That hasn't happened. In fact, people are reading more books than ever. *(People can buy books in stores and over the Internet.)* Libraries are changing to meet the needs of today's visitors. Libraries still stock the latest books and magazines. Today's libraries also provide a free place for people to check their E-mail and use the Internet.

Main Idea 7

Say, "A newspaper headline often expresses, or at least hints at, the main idea of a story. Listen as I read these brief news items. Then I will read three headlines. You tell me which one best expresses the main idea of the story."

1. Armstrong Junior High won last night's track meet with some great running. Armstrong beat Collins 85-47 at City Field on a warm evening. The Armstrong Lancers took first place in all but one of the running events.

   a. *(Armstrong Runs Away with Victory)*
   b. Track Meet Held Last Night
   c. Collins Visits City Field

2. The Celebrations Bakery burned to the ground yesterday afternoon. Firefighters battled for three hours but nothing could be saved. "The bakery has been in my family for 70 years," the owner said. He also said the bakery would be rebuilt.

   a. Bakery Owner Not Sure How Fire Started
   b. *(70-year-old Bakery Lost in Fire)*
   c. Firefighters Lacked Proper Equipment

3. One hundred years ago farming was the most popular job in America. Over five million people made their living from growing food. Today more people are involved in sales than any other type of job. Farming is not even in the top ten anymore.

   a. *(American Job Needs Change in Last 100 Years)*
   b. America Is Producing Less Food Than 100 Years Ago
   c. More Sales People Are Needed in American Companies

4. Do you think your school year is long? Most American students spend 180 days in the classroom. In China it's a whole different story. Chinese children go to school 251 days a year. That's more than any other nation. Japan is a close second. Their kids go to school 243 days a year.

   a. Japan Second to China in School Attendance
   b. American Students Aren't as Smart as Chinese Students
   c. *(Chinese Students Have More School Days Than Any Other Nation)*

Main Idea 8

Say, "Listen as I read each news story. Then tell me a headline that would tell the main idea of each story."

(Note: Answers will vary.)

1. A big crowd at West Speedway saw some great races last night. The second annual Lawn Mower Rally Cup was a big hit with the spectators. These aren't just ordinary lawn mowers. They can reach speeds of up to 30 miles per hour. You could get your grass cut in no time with these machines! *(Lawn mowers Race to Victory at Lawn Mower Rally Cup)*

2. The City Council welcomed its newest member last night. Loretta Stanley, who won last fall's election, joined the council. Her campaign against Councilman Burns was often heated. Burns said in public that he didn't like Ms. Stanley at all. Before the meeting, Ms. Stanley took the podium to say a few words. "I'm happy to be here tonight, and I'd like to thank everyone for their support," she said. "I know some nasty things were said during the election, but I want to put that all behind us. I'm looking forward to doing great things for our city." *(Loretta Stanley Joins City Council after Heated Campaign)*

3. A rare animal made its first public appearance at Armstrong Zoo this morning. Chalky is a nearly all-white giraffe. An albino giraffe would be completely white, but Chalky has some spots on his legs. The zoo's director says Chalky has a rare disorder that keeps most of his skin uncolored. Chalky will be on loan to the zoo for three months. Come out and say "Hi" to our new, unusual friend. *(Unusual Giraffe Appears at Armstrong Zoo)*

Main Idea 9

Say, "Main ideas usually support an overall topic. Think of a topic as a book and main ideas as chapters within a book. A topic is something general and large. I'm going to read you some phrases that could represent main ideas of paragraphs. You tell me what the overall topic would be."

1. Main Ideas:
   How to use a keyboard
   How to adjust the monitor
   How to safely shut down
   How to use a mouse
   (using a computer)

2. Main Ideas:
   Speak clearly.
   Prepare your notes.
   Do research.
   Practice in front of a mirror.
   (preparing for a speech)

3. Main Ideas:
   Exercise three times a week.
   Eat five fruits or vegetables a day.
   Avoid foods high in calories and sugar.
   Drink eight glasses of water a day.
   (ways to stay healthy)

4. Main Ideas:
   Read instructions.
   Answer questions you know first.
   Eliminate incorrect responses in multiple
     choice questions.
   Review answers.
   (taking a test)

5. Main Ideas:
   Know how to operate your camera.
   Use the correct film.
   Choose interesting subjects.
   Wait for the right moment.
   (taking photographs)

6. Main Ideas:
   Pick a topic.
   Do research.
   Write a rough draft.
   Proofread and correct your mistakes.
   (writing an essay or a report)

7. Main Ideas:
   Animals with spines
   Animals with scales
   Poisonous animals
   Animals with sharp teeth
   (animals and their defenses)

8. Main Ideas:
   Read instructions.
   Gather supplies.
   Form a hypothesis.
   Record your results.
   (doing a science experiment)

Differentiating Speakers' Purposes

Good listeners automatically change their listening style to meet different situations. One way to recognize when it's time to "switch listening gears" is to identify the purpose of the person who is speaking. Beyond recognizing an informal vs. formal listening situation, realizing why someone is speaking to you allows you to prepare yourself to listen in the most appropriate way.

There are three basic reasons for communication to occur. Introduce these types of communication and their characteristics to your students.

Entertainment
- Purpose is enjoyment or recreation
- Usually not just one-to-one communication; often occurs in a group setting or through the media
- Often an informal listening situation, but usually a passive one
- Includes listening to performances, watching movies, seeing shows

Information
- Purpose is to learn something new or hear directions
- Often occurs in a group situation but can be one-on-one
- Usually a formal listening situation requiring attention, concentration, and asking appropriate questions
- Includes listening to teachers, authority figures, and often parents

Social
- Purpose is to build relationships and get to know others
- Often is one-on-one, but also exists in group situations
- Usually an information listening situation that requires respect, attention, and conversation
- Includes communication with friends, family members, and people you are just getting to know

Differentiating Speakers' Purposes 1

Photocopy this page and give copies of the bottom half to your students.

Say, "People speak to us for many different reasons. Listen as I tell you about each of the three basic reasons we listen to others. Write the names of people or types of people that take part in each kind of communication. An example is given for each type."

Entertainment: This type of communication is for fun or enjoyment. It often involves listening to or watching others.

Information: This type of communication is for learning something new or hearing directions. It involves listening carefully to what someone is saying and asking appropriate questions.

Social: This type of communication is for getting to know people better and communicating with the important people in our lives. It involves paying attention and having good conversations.

- -

Entertainment	Information	Social
1. _pop singer_	1. _teacher_	1. _best friend_
2. _____	2. _____	2. _____
3. _____	3. _____	3. _____
4. _____	4. _____	4. _____
5. _____	5. _____	5. _____
6. _____	6. _____	6. _____

Differentiating Speakers' Purposes 2

Photocopy this page and give copies of the right half to your students.

Say, "Listen as I give you a list of speakers. Think about what would be the most likely reason for each person to be speaking. Put a check in the correct column for each person."

(Note: Answers are listed next to speaker: E for entertainment, I for Information, and S for social.)

Speaker		Entertainment	Information	Social
1. your favorite actor *(E)*	1.			
2. your big brother *(S)*	2.			
3. school principal *(I)*	3.			
4. your best friend *(S)*	4.			
5. kid who asks you to play on his soccer team *(S)*	5.			
6. your soccer coach *(I)*	6.			
7. crossing guard *(I)*	7.			
8. magician who performs at your school *(E)*	8.			
9. substitute teacher *(I)*	9.			
10. singer you hear on the radio *(E)*	10.			
11. your grandfather *(S)*	11.			
12. librarian *(I)*	12.			
13. TV news reporter *(I)*	13.			

Differentiating Speakers' Purposes 3

Say, "Different listening situations require you to act in different ways. I'm going to read some listening situations for you. First tell me what the speaker's (or group's) purpose is for communicating: entertainment, information, or social. Then show me how you would be a good listener in each situation. Explain exactly what you would do in order to be a good listener."

Situation	Speaker's Purpose	Appropriate Behavior
1. Your teacher is explaining a very complicated homework assignment.	*(information)*	*(sitting up straight in chair, quiet, listening carefully, taking notes)*
2. A band is playing for a school assembly.	*(entertainment)*	*(sitting comfortably, staying quiet, moving to the music)*
3. Your mother is giving you clear directions for cleaning your room. She wants you to have it done in an hour.	*(information)*	*(standing up straight, making eye contact, asking questions about things you don't understand)*
4. A friend is asking you what you did over the weekend.	*(social)*	*(keeping eye contact, standing/sitting comfortably, paying attention)*
5. A friend is telling you that her dog ran away. She seems very sad.	*(social)*	*(standing/sitting comfortably, keeping eye contact, paying attention, showing concern)*
6. You go with your parents to see a comedian perform on stage.	*(entertainment)*	*(laughing, relaxing, paying attention, enjoying yourself)*
7. A police officer visits your school to talk about bicycle safety.	*(information)*	*(sit/stand up straight, be quiet, listen carefully, ask appropriate questions)*

Differentiating Speakers' Purposes 4

Say, "Sometimes things happen that make it hard for us to listen carefully. These things are called 'distractions.' Distractions can occur in almost any kind of situation. I'm going to read you some situations. Then I'll read two things that are happening in the situation. You tell me which one is the distraction. Then tell me how you could stop the distraction or keep it from bothering you."

1. Your teacher is explaining what you need to study for tomorrow's reading test.

   a. The person who sits behind you keeps kicking your chair.
   b. Your teacher is speaking in a clear voice.
   (Distraction: The person who sits behind you keeps kicking your chair.
   How to stop it: Ask him to stop kicking your chair, Move your chair away from him.)

2. The high school band is playing a concert for your school in the gym.

   a. The band is playing a song you really like.
   b. It's very cold in the gym and you have on a short-sleeved shirt.
   (Distraction: It's very cold in the gym and you have on a short-sleeved shirt.
   How to stop it: Ask your teacher if you can go get a sweater or jacket.)

3. Your mom is asking you to explain the grade you got in math on your report card.

   a. Your little brother is standing behind her making goofy faces.
   b. She's talking very calmly and seems really concerned about you.
   (Distraction: Your little brother is standing behind her making goofy faces.
   How to stop it: Ask him to stop making faces at you, Turn so you can't see your brother,
   Ask your mom if you can talk to her in private.)

4. You're listening to the radio and your favorite song is on.

   a. Your dad is vacuuming in the other room.
   b. You're listening on your brand new CD player with built-in radio.
   (Distraction: Your dad is vacuuming in the other room.
   How to stop it: Ask him to stop vacuuming, Close the door, Move to another room.)

5. You're talking to a friend about what he's going to do this summer.

   a. Your friend is telling you about where he's going on his family vacation.
   b. Your friend keeps shuffling his feet and looking all around as he talks.
   (Distraction: Your friend keeps shuffling his feet and looking all around as he talks.
   How to stop it: Ask him to look at you when he talks, Ask him to stand still.)

6. Your uncle has been taking guitar lessons and he is playing in front of people for the first time.

   a. Your uncle has a really nice, brand new guitar.
   b. Your uncle keeps hitting wrong notes and doesn't play very well.
   (Distraction: Your uncle keeps hitting wrong notes and doesn't play very well.
   How to stop it: Move away so you can't hear him, Just pretend he's doing well so you don't hurt
   his feelings.)

Differentiating Speakers' Purposes 5

Say, "You know that people speak for entertainment, information, and social reasons. Sometimes what you hear can be for more than one reason. Listen to each situation. Choose two reasons why each message might be communicated."

1. A really cool commercial for a new kind of car. *(entertainment, information)*

2. You get home from school and your dad tells you a really funny joke. *(entertainment, social)*

3. You visit your grandpa and he tells you some interesting stories about how things were when he was growing up. *(social, information)*

4. A famous musician visits your school. He plays all kinds of drums from different countries and tells you about them as he plays. *(entertainment, information)*

5. Your big brother is in a high school play. Your whole family goes to see it. *(social, entertainment)*

6. You watch an exciting show on TV about the Amazon Rain Forest and the kinds of animals that live there. *(entertainment, information)*

7. Your dad shows you how he changes the oil on the car and tells you how the engine works. *(social, information)*

8. You go to your friend's place and he shows you his huge rock collection. He tells you about all the different kinds of rocks he has. *(social, information)*

Grammar

Most direct instruction for grammar in the classroom uses a written format. Some young students, though, need extra practice in paying attention to the grammar in what they hear before they can apply their grammar skills to what they read or write. This unit parallels the grammar skills taught in grades 3 through 5, but only in a listening format. The goal of these activities is to sharpen listening skills as well as to reinforce basic grammar skills.

Present the stimuli at a normal speaking rate. If a child has trouble answering, slow your presentation rate and increase the pause between items.

Grammar 1

Say, "A sentence must tell a complete thought. It must tell who or what the sentence is about, and it must tell what is or what happens. Listen carefully. Tell me if what I say is a complete sentence."

1. Tulips and daffodils bloom in the spring. *(yes)*

2. slimy green Jell-O for lunch today *(no)*

3. Janey saw a rabbit hiding under the bush. *(yes)*

4. Jack wants to write a funny story. *(yes)*

5. will go to the dentist next Friday *(no)*

6. rake the leaves and mow the grass *(no)*

7. I baby-sit my little sister after school. *(yes)*

8. will arrive in the afternoon *(no)*

9. Tina found her slippers under the bed. *(yes)*

10. had a scowl on his wrinkled face *(no)*

11. builds strength, stamina, and agility *(no)*

12. Mrs. Parker will be our guest speaker today. *(yes)*

13. Thousands of bees live and work inside one hive. *(yes)*

14. struggling up the stairs and gasping for breath *(no)*

15. Windmills help people use wind power as an energy source. *(yes)*

16. lizards, snakes, turtles, crocodiles, and alligators *(no)*

17. The dance will be Wednesday after school. *(yes)*

18. The bell rang loudly and interrupted our quiet reading time. *(yes)*

19. ate popcorn at the movies last night *(no)*

20. We can try out for the play on Monday or Tuesday. *(yes)*

21. beside the old pine tree next to the gate *(no)*

22. Neither Jason nor Jenny has been to the library yet. *(yes)*

23. Tornadoes are violent storms that can appear suddenly. *(yes)*

24. walking home after school one day last week *(no)*

25. piled high with fresh produce at the market *(no)*

Grammar 2

Say, "There are four kinds of sentences. A statement tells something. A question asks something. A command tells someone to do something. An exclamation shows strong feeling. Listen carefully to what I say. Then tell me what kind of sentence it is."

(Note: Some students may need a cue card to do this task easily. The cue card should list the four sentence types and their brief definitions. Also, use the same terminology your students are learning in their textbooks. Beginning in grade 5, students may refer to the four sentence types as declarative, interrogative, imperative, and exclamatory sentences.)

1. Where did you get your ticket? *(question/interrogative)*

2. Turn out the lights, please. *(command/imperative)*

3. That's a brilliant idea, Jeremy! *(exclamation/exclamatory)*

4. Who knows the answer to number 11? *(question/interrogative)*

5. Brian mowed the lawn after school. *(statement/declarative)*

6. What a fabulous day! *(exclamation/exclamatory)*

7. Did you go to the football game last night? *(question/interrogative)*

8. I liked your poem about butterflies. *(statement/declarative)*

9. Mount Everest is dangerous to climb. *(statement/declarative)*

10. Use water that's room temperature in the recipe. *(command/imperative)*

11. Have you ever built a sandcastle? *(question/interrogative)*

12. I need to choose a topic for my research report. *(statement/declarative)*

13. What time are you picking me up? *(question/interrogative)*

14. Quick! Get the fire extinguisher! *(exclamation/exclamatory)*

15. Our puppy isn't potty-trained yet. *(statement/declarative)*

16. Can penguins fly? *(question/interrogative)*

17. Do your homework before playing video games. *(command/imperative)*

18. Do you want to go to a movie with me? *(question/interrogative)*

19. It is so hot in here! *(exclamation/exclamatory)*

20. Dinner will be ready in a half hour. *(statement/declarative)*

21. I can't remember where I put my glasses. *(statement/declarative)*

22. Turn the music down, please. *(command/imperative)*

23. Look out below! *(exclamation/exclamatory)*

24. I want to sing in the chorus next year. *(statement/declarative)*

25. Did you remember to send Grandpa a postcard? *(question/interrogative)*

Grammar 3

Say, "The subject of a sentence tells who or what the sentence is about. Listen carefully. Tell me the complete subject for each sentence I say."

(Note: For students who can easily identify the complete subject, revise the directions above so that your students identify the simple subject (the noun), shown here in boldfaced type.)

1. *(The last **bus**)* has already left the school.

2. *(Jon's youngest **sister**)* broke her leg in-line skating.

3. *(The bake **sale**)* was a huge success!

4. *(A pig's **tail**)* is short and curly.

5. *(Jillian's soccer **team**)* won the game last night.

6. *(Many beautiful **flowers**)* grow in Hawaii.

7. *(My next-door **neighbor**)* raked the leaves in his yard.

8. *(Mr. Truman's science **experiments**)* are fun to do!

9. *(That newspaper **article**)* contains many opinions.

10. *(An interesting **character** in the story)* is Mrs. Puffindorf.

11. *(My oldest **brother**)* makes dinner once a week.

12. *(Some female **turtles**)* lay at least a hundred eggs at a time.

13. *(A dry desert **climate**)* is typical of many Southwestern states.

14. Since last year, *(Abby's curly **hair**)* has grown three inches.

15. *(**Farmers** in California)* grow most of the food that people in the U.S. eat.

16. After June 1st, *(the city **pool**)* will open at 8:00 a.m.

17. *(Some **students**)* chose to plant flowers for extra credit in science.

18. One lazy afternoon, *(several hungry **ants**)* interrupted our picnic.

19. *(The girls' basketball **team**)* will meet in the gym after school.

20. Of the three routes home, *(the old gravel **road**)* is usually the fastest.

21. For the holidays, *(our entire **family**)* will be going to Texas.

22. Because of the storm, *(many **homes and businesses**)* were without power.

23. *(A large amount of **rainfall**)* can cause the Mississippi River to flood.

24. During the 1800s, *(many **pioneers**)* traveled to the far West.

25. While you were gone, *(the new **principal**)* visited our classroom.

Grammar 4

Say, "The predicate of a sentence tells what is or what is happening. Listen carefully. Tell me the complete predicate for each sentence I say."

(Note: For students who can easily identify the complete predicate, revise the directions above so that your students identify the simple predicate (the verb), shown here in boldfaced type.)

1. Kim's older brother (**works** *at Pete's Diner*).

2. Our teacher this year (**is** *Ms. Brown*).

3. Robert (**dyed** *his hair purple*).

4. We (**admire** *the mountain climber's courage*).

5. My dog, Ralph, (**likes** *to play fetch*).

6. Our class (**went** *to the zoo yesterday*).

7. Timothy (**asked** *if he could have some more popcorn*).

8. People (**use** *water every day when they bathe, cook, and clean*).

9. Nicholas and Madelyn (**chose** *players for their teams*).

10. The school cafeteria (**offers** *meals at breakfast and lunch*).

11. Matt's baseball team (**won** *first place in the state finals*).

12. The candidates (**battled** *to win votes in the recent election*).

13. The pastry chef (**measured** *the ingredients for the cake*).

14. People all over the world (**are working** *to fight air pollution*).

15. My cousin Kim (**teaches** *first grade at Jefferson Elementary*).

16. The Colorado River (**flows** *through the Grand Canyon*).

17. Brianne's stepdad (**is baking** *cookies for the bake sale*).

18. Food, clothing, and shelter (**are** *the basic needs of all people*).

19. The President of the United States (**lives** *in the White House*).

20. Kate's grandma and grandpa (**go** *to Florida every winter*).

21. My friends and I (**swim** *almost every day in the summer*).

22. Many of Albert Einstein's inventions (**changed** *the world forever*).

23. Jennelle's grandmother (**reads** *the newspaper every day after breakfast*).

24. My older sister (**blames** *me for getting ketchup on her new sweater*).

25. More and more people (**consider** *E-mail an important communication tool*).

Grammar 5

Say, "A common noun names a person, place or thing, such as *sailboat*. A proper noun names a particular person, place or thing, such as *Abraham Lincoln*. Tell me whether each noun I say is a common noun or a proper noun."

1. country *(common)*
2. Alabama *(proper)*
3. Harry Potter *(proper)*
4. Rocky Mountains *(proper)*
5. mile *(common)*
6. adjective *(common)*
7. Dr. Morris *(proper)*
8. citizen *(common)*
9. buffalo *(common)*
10. Colorado River *(proper)*
11. 41st Street *(proper)*
12. circumference *(common)*
13. ballot *(common)*
14. Grand Canyon National Park *(proper)*
15. centimeter *(common)*
16. Anne Frank *(proper)*

Say, "A singular noun names one person, place or thing, such as *forest*. A plural noun names more than one person, place or thing, such as *trees* or *children*. Tell me whether each noun I say is singular or plural."

1. eagle *(singular)*
2. novel *(singular)*
3. valleys *(plural)*
4. degree *(singular)*
5. Americans *(plural)*
6. feet *(plural)*
7. neighborhood *(singular)*
8. windshield *(singular)*
9. leaves *(plural)*
10. protein *(singular)*
11. planet *(singular)*
12. lullabies *(plural)*
13. natural resources *(plural)*
14. people *(plural)*
15. ounce *(singular)*
16. glacier *(singular)*

Grammar 6

Say, "Tell me whether each sentence I say uses the present tense, the past tense, or the future tense."

1. Carlos will collect eggs from the chickens. *(future)*

2. Some whole numbers do not divide evenly. *(present)*

3. A river often flows through the bottom of a valley. *(present)*

4. My dad ordered 16 boxes of Girl Scout Cookies. *(past)*

5. A premature baby was born before its due date. *(past)*

6. Juanita will move to Arizona next month. *(future)*

7. Seven times five equals 35. *(present)*

8. A rock that is dropped in a glass of water will sink. *(future)*

9. People watched television for the first time in 1936. *(past)*

10. Pedro met the author of his favorite book at the mall. *(past)*

11. You can't see air, but you can feel it when the wind blows. *(present)*

12. Some people believe that life exists on other planets. *(present)*

13. Angel will return her library books after dinner. *(future)*

14. Fish use their fins to help them steer and balance in the water. *(present)*

15. A tadpole will develop into a frog in about 11 weeks. *(future)*

16. Beth will write a narrative to tell about her experiences at camp. *(future)*

17. Many pilgrims got sick or died during their first winter in America. *(past)*

18. That advertisement gives a lot of facts about pollution. *(present)*

19. We will talk about how new inventions change our lives. *(future)*

20. Rice, wheat, and corn are important grain crops. *(present)*

21. India makes more movies than Hollywood. *(present)*

22. You'll see many historic sights in Washington, D.C. *(future)*

23. Over the years, many people have migrated to the U.S. *(past)*

24. The weather forecaster said it will be hot and humid tomorrow. *(future)*

25. Many Middle Eastern countries export crude oil. *(present)*

Grammar 7

Say, "I will say a sentence in the past tense. Tell me whether the sentence is correct or incorrect. If it is incorrect, please say the sentence correctly."

1. Alonzo **had brung** his book report. *(incorrect; Alonzo brought/had brought his book report.)*

2. Marcus **standed** in line. *(incorrect; Marcus stood in line.)*

3. Emma **did** a somersault. *(correct)*

4. Haley **has begun** delivering newspapers. *(correct)*

5. Lindsey **has wrote** a note. *(incorrect; Lindsey wrote/has written a note.)*

6. The eagle **flew** over our heads. *(correct)*

7. Our school **has chose** a mascot. *(incorrect; Our school chose/has chosen a mascot.)*

8. Tyler **rided** his bike to school. *(incorrect; Tyler rode his bike to school.)*

9. Olivia **has lent** me her new CD. *(correct)*

10. Kris **has took** swimming lessons. *(incorrect; Kris took/has taken swimming lessons.)*

11. Grandpa **has drank** all the milk. *(incorrect; Grandpa drank/has drunk all the milk.)*

12. Cameron **wore** his new baseball uniform. *(correct)*

13. The bird's nest **has fallen** out of the tree. *(correct)*

14. They **have knew** about the party. *(incorrect; They knew/have known about the party.)*

15. Kaylie **winned** the science contest. *(incorrect; Kaylie won the science contest.)*

16. The choir **sang** a beautiful song. *(correct)*

17. Noah **has came** to help us. *(incorrect; Noah came/has come to help us.)*

18. Our tomato plants **have grown** three inches. *(correct)*

19. Sophie **falled** and **broked** her arm. *(incorrect; Sophie fell and broke her arm.)*

20. I **seen** that movie already. *(incorrect; I saw/have seen that movie already.)*

21. Antonio **has catched** a cold. *(incorrect; Antonio caught/has caught a cold.)*

22. Jade **throwed** three strikes in a row! *(incorrect; Jade threw three strikes in a row!)*

23. We almost **froze** while waiting for the bus. *(correct)*

24. I **have gave** you my answer. *(incorrect; I gave/have given you my answer.)*

25. Margaret **has lost** her favorite earrings. *(correct)*

Grammar 8

Say, "The subject and the verb of a sentence must match. They must both be either singular or plural. Listen to each sentence. Tell me whether the sentence is correct or incorrect. If it is incorrect, please say the sentence correctly."

1. **History** and **math is** easy for me. *(incorrect; History and math are easy for me.)*

2. **Chelsea** and **I are** lab partners. *(correct)*

3. The character's **mood were** happy. *(incorrect; The character's mood was happy.)*

4. **Blake will see** llamas when he goes to Peru. *(correct)*

5. **We pays** taxes to the government. *(incorrect; We pay taxes to the government.)*

6. **Jeff** and **I helped** Mr. Pope at his pet store. *(correct)*

7. The **pizza will be** here at 1:00. *(correct)*

8. **Books uses** words to tell a story. *(incorrect; Books use words to tell a story.)*

9. Most **bats will eats** insects. *(incorrect; Most bats will eat insects.)*

10. **Ronald Reagan was** the oldest elected U.S. President. *(correct)*

11. All **leaves has** three layers. *(incorrect; All leaves have three layers.)*

12. **Sara were** on the Internet all night! *(incorrect; Sara was on the Internet all night!)*

13. Which restaurant **will we goes** to? *(incorrect; Which restaurant will we go to?)*

14. **Trees** and **plants grow** from seeds and nuts. *(correct)*

15. There **is** six time **zones** in the U.S. *(incorrect; There are six time zones in the U.S.)*

16. **Bo** and **Lee will go** to the Chinese New Year Parade. *(correct)*

17. **Coyotes is** very good hunters. *(incorrect; Coyotes are very good hunters.)*

18. **Lauren have written** a letter to the editor. *(incorrect; Lauren has written a letter to the editor.)*

19. **Will Jon** and **Lyn make** a graph to go with their report? *(correct)*

20. **Susan B. Anthony fought** for voting rights for women. *(correct)*

21. **Is they going** to be at the concert? *(incorrect; Are they going to be at the concert?)*

22. **Samantha is** always nervous before a test. *(correct)*

23. **Julia will writes** her report on otters. *(incorrect; Julia will write her report on otters.)*

24. **Has they been** to the new pool yet? *(incorrect; Have they been to the new pool yet?)*

25. **Jennifer hurt** her foot while running the race. *(correct)*

Grammar 9

Say, "The subject and the verb of a sentence must match. They must both be either singular or plural. Listen to each sentence. Tell me whether the sentence is correct or incorrect. If it is incorrect, please say the sentence correctly."

1. Our **dog do** not **look** like her mother. *(incorrect; Our dog does not look like her mother.)*

2. **Water is** an important natural resource. *(correct)*

3. The **strawberries was**n't ripe yet. *(incorrect; The strawberries weren't ripe yet.)*

4. The **recycling center will be** open until 5:00 today. *(correct)*

5. **Anna** always **take** good notes. *(incorrect; Anna always takes good notes.)*

6. **Sammy had** his picture **taken** yesterday. *(correct)*

7. **Spaghetti is** easy to make and delicious too. *(correct)*

8. **I is going** out of town this weekend. *(incorrect; I am going out of town this weekend.)*

9. My **mom will brings** the treats. *(incorrect; My mom will bring the treats.)*

10. **Pioneers used** horses to pull their covered wagons. *(correct)*

11. **Ian like** to do his math homework first. *(incorrect; Ian likes to do his math homework first.)*

12. That **movie were** hilarious! *(incorrect; That movie was hilarious!)*

13. **Amber will takes** Spanish next year. *(incorrect; Amber will take Spanish next year.)*

14. A **dinosaur is** an example of an extinct animal. *(correct)*

15. **Do Dorie** still **have** your earrings? *(incorrect; Does Dorie still have your earrings?)*

16. **Justin will try** not to scratch his poison ivy. *(correct)*

17. **Josie** and **Jill keeps** their room clean. *(incorrect; Josie and Jill keep their room clean.)*

18. **Erik** and **Kevin was** at the hospital. *(incorrect; Erik and Kevin were at the hospital.)*

19. This **computer will run** the new program. *(correct)*

20. My **cow was** three years old when she had her first calf. *(correct)*

21. **Victor will describes** the setting. *(incorrect; Victor will describe the setting.)*

22. Frozen **yogurt is** lower in fat and calories than ice cream. *(correct)*

23. **Will you buys** some stamps for me? *(incorrect; Will you buy some stamps for me?)*

24. **Alex have found** the flashlight. *(incorrect; Alex has found the flashlight.)*

25. **Did you know** that an animal's color can help it survive? *(correct)*

Grammar 10

Say, "The subject and the verb of a sentence must match. They must both be either singular or plural. Listen to each sentence. Tell me whether the sentence is correct or incorrect. If it is incorrect, please say the sentence correctly."

1. A **horse** and a **dog is** mammals. *(incorrect; A horse and a dog are mammals.)*

2. **Daniel made** the honor roll at school. *(correct)*

3. **Hannah** and **Emily has found** their keys. *(incorrect; Hannah and Emily have found their keys.)*

4. My **uncle will try** to climb Mount Everest this year. *(correct)*

5. **Do you know** that whales have great vision? *(correct)*

6. The **Eiffel Tower was built** over 100 years ago. *(correct)*

7. **Keesha** and **Darnell are looking** for starfish on the beach. *(correct)*

8. Logan's **shoes is** in the closet. *(incorrect; Logan's shoes are in the closet.)*

9. The **jury will decides** the verdict. *(incorrect; The jury will decide the verdict.)*

10. The ballet **dancer took** a slow, deep bow. *(correct)*

11. The **captain** and the **crew is** ready. *(incorrect; The captain and the crew are ready.)*

12. The **assignment were due** yesterday. *(incorrect; The assignment was due yesterday.)*

13. **Steve** and **Rita will meets** at the library. *(incorrect; Steve and Rita will meet at the library.)*

14. When they're born, polar bear **cubs** only **weigh** about a pound. *(correct)*

15. A hummingbird's **wings is** strong. *(incorrect; A hummingbird's wings are strong.)*

16. **We will win** the game if Ted makes this free throw. *(correct)*

17. **Dad enjoy** listening to jazz music. *(incorrect; Dad enjoys listening to jazz music.)*

18. **Has you read** your E-mail yet? *(incorrect; Have you read your E-mail yet?)*

19. Almost **two-thirds** of your body **are** water. *(incorrect; Almost two-thirds of your body is water.)*

20. Before the game started, the **crowd sang** the "Star Spangled Banner." *(correct)*

Grammar 11

Say, "An adjective tells information about a noun. It might answer the question *how many* or *what kind*. The little words *a*, *an*, and *the* are also adjectives. Tell me each adjective in what I say."

(Note: If your students have trouble identifying the adjectives, have them find the noun first and then listen for words that describe that noun.)

1. under the shaggy carpet *(the, shaggy)*

2. a tropical jungle *(a, tropical)*

3. some wild animals *(some, wild)*

4. up the steep hill *(the, steep)*

5. favorite short story *(favorite, short)*

6. a rough surface *(a, rough)*

7. sharp teeth and loud roars *(sharp, loud)*

8. in the far northern regions *(the, far, northern)*

9. an exciting fireworks display *(an, exciting, fireworks)*

10. through the thick grassy plains *(the, thick, grassy)*

11. a big fat juicy earthworm *(a, big, fat, juicy)*

12. a long green body *(a, long, green)*

13. on the large outdoor stage *(the, large, outdoor)*

14. a slow chemical change *(a, slow, chemical)*

15. the tired and hungry hikers *(the, tired, hungry)*

16. during several long hard battles *(several, long, hard)*

17. on a damp and dreary afternoon *(a, damp, dreary)*

18. the swift river current *(the, swift, river)*

19. many silly circus acts *(many, silly, circus)*

20. two furry little kittens *(two, furry, little)*

21. the enormous clear blue sea *(the, enormous, clear, blue)*

22. one cold crisp winter morning *(one, cold, crisp, winter)*

23. four or five small plastic cups *(four, five, small, plastic)*

24. an early morning exercise class *(an, early, morning, exercise)*

25. the beautiful red, orange, and gold leaves *(the, beautiful, red, orange, gold)*

Grammar 12

Say, "Listen to what I say about comparing things. Tell me whether the sentence is correct or incorrect. If it is incorrect, please say the sentence correctly."

1. An artery is **more larger** than a vein. *(incorrect; An artery is larger than a vein.)*

2. Explorers wanted to find the **most shortest** route to China. *(incorrect; Explorers wanted to find the shortest route to China.)*

3. These pioneers chose an **easier** trail to head west. *(correct)*

4. Jenna is the **most friendliest** person in the class. *(incorrect; Jenna is the most friendly/friendliest person in the class.)*

5. This book is the **most interesting** one. *(correct)*

6. A freezer is **more colder** than a refrigerator. *(incorrect; A freezer is colder than a refrigerator.)*

7. The Nile River is **more longer** than the Mississippi River. *(incorrect; The Nile River is longer than the Mississippi River.)*

8. The elephant is the **most biggest** animal at the zoo. *(incorrect; The elephant is the biggest animal at the zoo.)*

9. A butterfly is **more colorful** than a bee. *(correct)*

10. It is **more wetter** in a rain forest than in a desert. *(incorrect; It is wetter in a rain forest than in a desert.)*

11. A novel is usually **longer** than an essay. *(correct)*

12. Hummingbirds are the **most smallest** birds of all. *(incorrect; Hummingbirds are the smallest birds of all.)*

13. Popcorn is a **healthier** snack food than potato chips. *(correct)*

14. Karen asked for the **thinnest** slice of pizza. *(correct)*

15. The Sun is the **most closest** star to the Earth. *(The Sun is the closest star to the Earth.)*

16. This room is the **most darkest** in the house. *(This room is the darkest in the house.)*

17. The Sears Tower is one of the **most tallest** buildings in the world. *(incorrect; The Sears Tower is one of the tallest buildings in the world.)*

18. Harriet Tubman was the **most famous** conductor on the Underground Railroad. *(correct)*

19. My sister's suitcase is **more heavier** than mine. *(incorrect; My sister's suitcase is heavier than mine.)*

20. Pluto is the **farthest** planet from the Sun. *(correct)*

Adjectives: Comparatives and Superlatives
100% Listening – Intermediate

Grammar 13

Say, "Listen to what I say about comparing things. Tell me whether the sentence is correct or incorrect. If it is incorrect, please say the sentence correctly."

1. An ocean is **more deeper** than a river. *(incorrect; An ocean is deeper than a river.)*

2. Pretty Boy is the **fastest** horse on the ranch. *(correct)*

3. A pig's tail is **more curlier** than a cow's tail. *(incorrect; A pig's tail is curlier than a cow's tail.)*

4. That's the **most prettiest** picture Shelby has ever painted. *(incorrect; That's the prettiest picture Shelby has ever painted.)*

5. My **youngest** brother, Roberto, is two years old. *(correct)*

6. We'll need some **stronger** rope to tie down the tarp. *(correct)*

7. This store needs **more wider** aisles to accommodate wheelchairs. *(incorrect; This store needs wider aisles to accommodate wheelchairs.)*

8. A pyramid is a **more older** structure than a city skyscraper. *(incorrect; A pyramid is an older structure than a city skyscraper.)*

9. Today is the **hottest** day so far this summer! *(correct)*

10. Mom said the **most dirtiest** socks in the pile were mine. *(incorrect; Mom said the dirtiest socks in the pile were mine.)*

11. Tom's **most happiest** times are when he's singing. *(incorrect; Tom's happiest times are when he's singing.)*

12. The **most littlest** spark can cause a forest fire. *(incorrect; The littlest spark can cause a forest fire.)*

13. Can you think of a **kinder** way to say that you're sorry? *(correct)*

14. This is the **most shiniest** coin in Maggie's collection. *(incorrect; This is the shiniest coin in Maggie's collection.)*

15. World War II was the **most destructive** war in human history. *(correct)*

16. I don't know anyone **more wiser** than Mr. Taylor. *(incorrect; I don't know anyone wiser than Mr. Taylor.)*

17. A crocodile's skin is much **more thicker** than a human's skin. *(incorrect; A crocodile's skin is much thicker than a human's skin.)*

18. A movie usually has **more better** special effects than a play. *(incorrect; A movie usually has better special effects than a play.)*

19. Because of its fight against pollution, Grand Hills is the **cleanest** town in the state. *(correct)*

20. A poisonous snake is **more dangerouser** than a frog. *(incorrect; A poisonous snake is more dangerous than a frog.)*

Grammar 14

Say, "Pay attention to the pronouns and the verbs in this sentence. They should both be either singular or plural. Tell me whether each sentence is correct or incorrect. If it is incorrect, please say the sentence correctly."

1. **They is going** to a meeting at 3:00. *(incorrect; They are going to a meeting at 3:00.)*

2. **We wants** another computer game. *(incorrect; We want another computer game.)*

3. **They is leaving** tomorrow for Ohio. *(incorrect; They are leaving tomorrow for Ohio.)*

4. **Is we getting** a new computer? *(incorrect; Are we getting a new computer?)*

5. **It smells** terrible! *(correct)*

6. **You** and **I has** matching outfits. *(incorrect; You and I have matching outfits.)*

7. **We take** turns setting the table for dinner. *(correct)*

8. **They thanks** us for helping them. *(incorrect; They thank/thanked us for helping them.)*

9. **Each** of us **do** our own laundry. *(incorrect; Each of us does our own laundry.)*

10. **I needs** a drink of water, please. *(incorrect; I need a drink of water, please.)*

11. **He has** an awesome rock collection. *(correct)*

12. **She are** on vacation this week. *(incorrect; She is on vacation this week.)*

13. **You is** my best friend. *(incorrect; You are my best friend.)*

14. **We has** to learn fractions in math. *(incorrect; We have to learn fractions in math.)*

15. **I am** in Mrs. Wagoner's fourth-grade class. *(correct)*

16. **We was checking** out books at the library. *(incorrect; We were checking out books at the library.)*

17. **She** and **I is going** to be late. *(incorrect; She and I are going to be late.)*

18. **Both** of us **is running** for class president. *(incorrect; Both of us are running for class president.)*

19. **She works** at Hilltop Park Children's Zoo. *(correct)*

20. **Do we has** some clean towels? *(incorrect; Do we have some clean towels?)*

21. **He is playing** a video game right now. *(correct)*

22. **Some** of my socks **is** missing. *(incorrect; Some of my socks are missing.)*

23. **He do** the laundry and **I do** the cooking. *(incorrect; He does the laundry and I do the cooking.)*

24. **She** and **Bailey get** new glasses every year. *(correct)*

25. **Each** of the puppies **were** black. *(incorrect; Each of the puppies was black.)*

Grammar 15

Say, "Pay attention to the pronouns in what I say. Tell me whether each sentence is correct or incorrect. If it is incorrect, please say the sentence correctly."

1. Take this poster to **him** and Gwen. *(correct)*

2. Ron and **myself** will introduce the speaker. *(incorrect; Ron and I will introduce the speaker.)*

3. Does Tim want to go fishing with **I**? *(incorrect; Does Tim want to go fishing with me?)*

4. **You** and I should work on our science project together. *(correct)*

5. **He** asked **you** and I to clean the kitchen. *(incorrect; He asked you and me to clean the kitchen.)*

6. Either **him** or James ate the last cookie. *(incorrect; Either he or James ate the last cookie.)*

7. **We** take piano lessons from Mrs. Melody. *(correct)*

8. **Them** will meet **us** after school. *(incorrect; They will meet us after school.)*

9. Logan and **me** will ride our bikes to practice. *(incorrect; Logan and I will ride our bikes to practice.)*

10. Please tell **her** that **you** will be late tomorrow. *(correct)*

11. My dog is afraid to stay by **hisself** during a storm. *(incorrect; My dog is afraid to stay by himself during a storm.)*

12. Don't forget to take **me** to school. *(correct)*

13. Does **her** have chickenpox? *(incorrect; Does she have chickenpox?)*

14. My brothers helped **theirselves** to my diary. *(incorrect; My brothers helped themselves to my diary.)*

15. **Him** and **me** watched a movie last night. *(incorrect; He and I watched a movie last night.)*

16. Karla made **herself** some popcorn for a snack. *(correct)*

17. Last night **us** heard a loud noise. *(incorrect; Last night we heard a loud noise.)*

18. Bring your permission slip to Mr. Witt or **myself**. *(incorrect; Bring your permission slip to Mr. Wong or me.)*

19. **Them** are my favorite jeans! *(incorrect; They/Those/These are my favorite jeans!)*

20. **I** know which I like best. *(correct)*

21. **It** was taller than any building I had ever seen! *(correct)*

22. Each baby has **their** own blanket. *(incorrect; Each baby has his/her own blanket.)*

23. **Whom** is using my pen? *(incorrect; Who is using my pen?)*

24. **Her** and me need to borrow some money. *(incorrect; She and I need to borrow some money.)*

25. The thunder was so loud, **it** woke **us** up. *(correct)*

Grammar 16

Say, "An adverb gives information about a verb. Adverbs tell *how, when,* or *where* something happens. Many adverbs end with *–ly*. Listen carefully. Tell me the adverb in each sentence I say."

1. Mix the vinegar and baking soda thoroughly. *(thoroughly)*

2. The author describes the setting clearly. *(clearly)*

3. The ballerina spun gracefully on her toes. *(gracefully)*

4. Keesha sings beautifully. *(beautifully)*

5. Martin did well on our last science quiz. *(well)*

6. The number nine can be divided evenly by the number three. *(evenly)*

7. Grizzly bears always hibernate in the winter. *(always)*

8. Savannah smiled shyly at her new baby-sitter. *(shyly)*

9. The 1920s are often referred to as "The Roaring 20s." *(often)*

10. Thomas accidentally dropped the book on his foot. *(accidentally)*

11. Many soldiers fought bravely in World War I. *(bravely)*

12. The audience clapped loudly at the end of the play. *(loudly)*

13. The assembly line was truly a great invention! *(truly)*

14. Patrick searched everywhere for his backpack. *(everywhere)*

15. Plan the outline of your paper as carefully as possible. *(carefully)*

16. Tomorrow our class will tour a recycling center. *(tomorrow)*

17. Juan and Cody decided to take the bus downtown. *(downtown)*

18. The dog barked fiercely at the stranger walking on the sidewalk. *(fiercely)*

19. The story's conflict is resolved slowly in the last two chapters. *(slowly)*

20. Kara checked her science experiment regularly and recorded any changes. *(regularly)*

21. Dry and windy conditions make it very difficult to put out a forest fire. *(very)*

22. Pony express riders rode swiftly from station to station. *(swiftly)*

23. The United States angrily declared war on Germany during World War II. *(angrily)*

24. Since the air is cold at the top of tall mountains, few plants can grow there. *(there)*

25. Millions of people sadly watched the funeral of Diana, Princess of Wales. *(sadly)*

Grammar 17

Say, "Listen to each sentence comparing things. Tell me whether each sentence is correct or incorrect. If it is incorrect, please say the sentence correctly."

1. Kirsten plays the clarinet **better** than I do. *(correct)*

2. Mark's journal is **more better** than Audrey's. *(incorrect; Mark's journal is better than Audrey's.)*

3. Ron stayed after school **more later** than Jim. *(incorrect; Ron stayed after school later than Jim.)*

4. Mrs. Finch's students cheered **loudest** of all the students. *(correct)*

5. Kim will finish her book **sooner** than Jason will. *(correct)*

6. Pam lives **closest** to me than to Bill. *(incorrect; Pam lives closer to me than to Bill.)*

7. A hurricane lasts **more longer** than a tornado. *(incorrect; A hurricane lasts longer than a tornado.)*

8. My mom wakes up **earlier** than the rest of us every day. *(correct)*

9. Bob gets his hair cut **oftener** than anyone I know! *(incorrect; Bob gets his hair cut more often than anyone I know!)*

10. An animal's fur grows **thicker** in the winter to keep it warm. *(correct)*

11. A cheetah runs **more faster** than an elephant. *(incorrect; A cheetah runs faster than an elephant.)*

12. I am **least tired** after playing basketball than my dad is. *(incorrect; I am less tired after playing basketball than my dad is.)*

13. Weather forecasters can predict a hurricane **earlier** than a tornado. *(correct)*

14. A kangaroo can jump **more higher** than a rabbit. *(incorrect; A kangaroo can jump higher than a rabbit.)*

15. Denise has taken Spanish **longest** than I have. *(incorrect; Denise has taken Spanish longer than I have.)*

16. Bats can see **better** at night than during the day. *(correct)*

17. The weather is even **worser** today than yesterday. *(incorrect; The weather is even worse today than yesterday.)*

18. Miles can swim **more quicker** than I can. *(incorrect; Miles can swim more quickly/quicker than I can.)*

19. Of everyone, Wayne sings the **most louder**. *(incorrect; Of everyone, Wayne sings the most loudly/loudest.)*

20. Flowers smell **more better** than grass. *(incorrect; Flowers smell better than grass.)*

Grammar 18

Say, "Tell me the prepositional phrases in each sentence I say."

(Note: If students have trouble locating prepositional phrases, provide a cue card listing common prepositions. Have more advanced students identify the preposition within each prepositional phrase, indicated here in boldfaced type.)

1. *(**Before** the Civil War)*, most *(**of** the factories)* were *(**in** the North)*.

2. Temperatures *(**in** the South)* rarely drop *(**below** zero)*.

3. Immigrants move *(**to** America)* *(**for** many different reasons)*.

4. The Cheyenne were one *(**of** many groups)* *(**of** Plains Indians)*.

5. The largest chain *(**of** mountains)* *(**in** the world)* is *(**under** the ocean)*.

6. *(**At** dawn)*, the farmer walked *(**across** the field)* *(**toward** the stream)*.

7. The Bill *(**of** Rights)* guarantees the basic freedoms *(**of** every American)*.

8. *(**Over** the summer)*, I read a book *(**about** slavery)* *(**in** the South)*.

9. Most *(**of** America's largest cities)* are *(**on** the ocean)* or *(**along** a river)*.

10. A valley is a low area *(**of** land)* *(**between** hills or mountains)*.

11. *(**Without** a doubt)*, you'll see lots *(**of** farmland)* when driving *(**through** Nebraska)*.

12. Cowboys moved cattle *(**from** Texas)* north *(**along** the Chisholm Trail)* *(**to** Kansas)*.

13. Different parts *(**of** the Midwest)* are good *(**for** different kinds)* *(**of** farms)*.

14. The world is filled *(**with** many different landforms)* and bodies *(**of** water)*.

15. *(**During** the California Gold Rush)*, thousands *(**of** people)* headed West to look *(**for** gold)*.

16. *(**After** the American Revolution)*, the U.S. earned its freedom *(**from** Britain)*.

17. We camped *(**near** a hot spring)* *(**at** Yellowstone National Park)* *(**in** Montana)*.

18. Most countries *(**in** the world today)* are members *(**of** the United Nations)*.

19. The President sat *(**behind** his desk)* *(**in** the Oval Office)* and spoke *(**to** the nation)*.

20. People *(**around** the world)* watched *(**in** horror)* as the World Trade Center fell *(**to** the ground)*.

Grammar 19

Say, "I'll tell you some sentences. Put the sentences together to make one sentence that tells all the information."

(Note: Your students' answers may vary.)

1. Lewis led an exploration trip.
   Clark led an exploration trip.
   (Lewis and Clark led an exploration trip.)

2. Thomas Edison invented the light bulb.
   Thomas Edison invented the phonograph.
   (Thomas Edison invented the light bulb and the phonograph.)

3. A male cardinal is about eight inches long.
   A male cardinal has bright red feathers.
   (A male cardinal is about eight inches long and has bright red feathers.)

4. The spectators began to cheer.
   They were loud.
   (The spectators began to cheer loudly.)

5. The sign tells the drivers to stop.
   The sign is on the side of the street.
   (The sign on the side of the street tells the drivers to stop.)

6. The Pacific is an ocean.
   It is the world's largest ocean.
   (The Pacific is the world's largest ocean.)

7. A hurricane is a type of storm.
   It is a very violent, dangerous storm.
   (A hurricane is a very violent, dangerous storm.)

8. Many Americans migrated during the 1800s.
   They migrated from east to west.
   (During the 1800s, Many Americans migrated from east to west.)

9. The Red Cross is a United Way agency.
   It is important.
   (The Red Cross is an important United Way agency.)

10. Giraffes have long tongues.
    Their tongues are black.
    They can clean their ears with their tongues.
    (Giraffes have long black tongues that they can use to clean their ears.)

11. We are going to a concert tonight.
    The concert is outside.
    (We are going to an outdoor concert tonight.)

Combining Sentences

12. Native Americans taught the settlers how to grow corn.
    They taught the settlers how to grow beans.
    They taught the settlers how to grow squash.
    (Native Americans taught the settlers how to grow corn, beans, and squash.)

13. I am writing an essay.
    My essay must be three pages long.
    The topic of my essay is "mummies."
    (I am writing a three-page essay about mummies.)

14. One war lasted just 38 minutes.
    It happened in 1896.
    It is the shortest war on record.
    (The shortest war on record occurred in 1896 and lasted just 38 minutes.)

15. The volunteers will mow lawns.
    The volunteers will rake leaves.
    The volunteers are students.
    (The student volunteers will mow lawns and rake leaves.)

16. Francis Scott Key wrote a song.
    The song is called "The Star Spangled Banner."
    He wrote this song in 1814.
    (Francis Scott Key wrote "The Star Spangled Banner" in 1814.)

17. George Washington was a President.
    He was the first President of the U.S.
    He was elected in 1789.
    (In 1789, George Washington became the first President of the U.S.)

18. Terrorists flew airplanes into two tall buildings.
    The buildings were in New York.
    This happened on September 11, 2001.
    (On September 11, 2001, terrorists flew airplanes into two tall buildings in New York.)

19. The American flag has 13 stripes.
    The stripes are red and white.
    The stripes represent the 13 original colonies.
    (The American flag has 13 red and white stripes that represent the 13 original colonies.)

20. Pony express riders were brave.
    Pony express riders rode long distances.
    They rode quickly.
    (Brave pony express riders rode long distances quickly.)

Combining Sentences
100% Listening – Intermediate   142

Inferences

Making inferences is an important learning and life skill for a student. It requires the application of prior knowledge to new information that is heard, seen, or read. It involves asking questions and combining new clues with prior knowledge to make a thoughtful deduction.

For most students, the mental process happens quickly despite its complexity. The second they encounter new information, their brains search for something familiar. Without realizing it, their brains kick into high gear to find a way to attach this new, unfamiliar information to something they already know.

Imagine this scenario. A child sees an ambulance parked in one of his neighbor's driveways. How does he infer what is happening?

- He identifies what he knows. He knows an elderly person lives across the street. He also knows older people often have health problems.

- He searches for clues about what's happening. He sees neighbors standing on the lawn and an ambulance parked in the driveway. The neighbors are serious and are talking quietly. He mentally asks questions like "Who is . . .?, What is . . .?, Where is . . .?, When is . . .?, Why did . . .?, and How did . . .?"

- He combines the clues with what he knows to make an inference. He thinks, "My neighbor is sick."

For some students, making inferences does not happen automatically or quickly. These students may have difficulty with reading and question comprehension, identifying relevant and irrelevant details, and justifying their opinions.

Use the items in this chapter to help your students practice making inferences. Post these important strategies on the wall before you begin and review them as you practice this skill.

1. **Listen for clues.** What things in the story will help you tell what is happening?

2. **Ask questions.** Who is this about? What is this about? Where is this happening? When is this happening? Why did this happen? How did this happen?

3. **Combine new clues with prior knowledge.** Then infer what is happening.

Inferences 1

Say, "Listen to what I say. Try to picture what is happening in your mind. Then answer the question."

1. Tyler put on his coat, boots, gloves, and hat. Then he went to the garage to get his toboggan. Where is Tyler going? *(sledding)*

2. The attendants closed the overhead bins and then prepared for takeoff. Where are the attendants? *(airplane)*

3. Hunter picks up his ball and puts the flag back into the hole. Then he carries his clubs to the next tee. Where is Hunter? *(golf course)*

4. Grace goes to the Lincoln Memorial and the Capitol Building. Then she takes a tour of the White House. Where is Grace? *(Washington, D.C.)*

5. Riley walks into the room and sits down. She looks at the jury. She wonders if they will find the man guilty or not guilty. Where is Riley? *(courtroom, courthouse)*

6. You are in a heated building that has a glass roof and sides. There are many plants in this building. Where are you? *(greenhouse)*

7. Isabel goes to the window and gives the check to the teller. Where is Isabel? *(bank)*

8. Jared gets into the elevator and goes to the third floor. He stops at the nurses' station to ask where Room 322 is. Where is Jared? *(hospital)*

9. You are tossing and turning because you are having a bad dream. Where are you? *(bed, bedroom)*

10. Miguel stands along the side of the road with his friends. They watch the floats go by and listen to the marching bands. Where are Miguel and his friends? *(parade)*

11. Elizabeth walks across the drawbridge and into the courtyard. Then she climbs the steps to her room in the tower. Where is Elizabeth? *(castle)*

12. You are in a country where you would find crocodiles, koalas, and kangaroos. Where are you? *(Australia)*

13. The man is standing on the stairs. He is not climbing the stairs, but he is still moving up. Where is the man? *(escalator)*

14. You buy a token and pass through the turnstile. Then you get into a vehicle that runs underground. Where are you? *(subway)*

15. Lucas gives his prescription to the man behind the counter. Where is Lucas? *(pharmacy, drugstore)*

Inferences 2

Say, "Listen to what I say. Try to picture what is happening in your mind. Then answer the question."

1. Mom drove home from work last night. This morning her car will not start. What could have happened? *(left lights on, battery is dead, mechanical problems)*

2. The phone rang twice, but when I picked up the receiver no one was there. What might have happened? *(person calling hung up, had wrong number)*

3. Shelly and Kim climbed the ladder up to the tree house. When they were ready to leave, they couldn't get down. What might have happened? *(ladder fell, someone took the ladder)*

4. Kyle worked on a jigsaw puzzle all week, but he never finished it. What could have happened? *(pieces missing, lost interest in the puzzle)*

5. As Morgan walked toward her house, she noticed that one of the front windows was broken. What could have happened? *(Someone hit a ball through the window, Someone tried to break in, A bird flew into the window.)*

6. Jessie put on an old pair of jeans. They fit around the waist, but they were too short. What could have happened? *(Jessie grew taller.)*

7. Evan was supposed to meet Ana at the restaurant at six o'clock. It's six-thirty and Ana isn't there yet. What could have happened? *(Ana's running late, She forgot about the meeting, Either Ana or Evan is at the wrong restaurant.)*

8. Sean drove home from school in a bad storm. Sean knew his parents were at home, but when he got there, the house was dark. What could have happened? *(electricity went out)*

9. Before he went to bed, Mr. Taylor set his garbage bags out on the curb. When he got up in the morning, the bags were torn and the garbage was strewn on the grass. What might have happened? *(raccoons or other animals got into garbage, vandalism)*

10. When Mya went to the store, she left a candle burning in her apartment. When she got home, a fire engine was in front of her apartment building. What might have happened? *(candle caught something on fire)*

11. Ali went ice-skating on her neighbor's pond yesterday. When she got to the pond today, there was a sign that said "No skating." What could have happened? *(warmed up and ice got too thin, neighbor doesn't want her skating on the pond)*

12. Jack left a message on Kevin's answering machine. He asked Kevin to call him back before eight. Kevin never called Jack back. What could have happened? *(Kevin didn't get the message, Kevin got home after eight so he didn't call, Kevin didn't want to call Jack back.)*

13. Yesterday you saw Cody practicing tricks on his skateboard. Today Cody has a cast on his leg. What could have happened? *(Cody broke his leg doing tricks on his skateboard.)*

Inferences 3

Say, "Listen to what I say. Try to picture what is happening in your mind. Then answer the question."

1. It was sleeting. Mr. Stimes suddenly lost control of his car and went off the road. Why do you think that happened? *(road was icy, driving too fast for conditions)*

2. Sarah was the last one in her family to take a shower this morning. When Sarah got in the shower, there was no hot water. Why do you think that happened? *(hot water used up by rest of family, water heater broken, pilot light out)*

3. Dave put some wet jeans into the dryer and then went out to play basketball. When he went back to get his clothes, they were still wet. Why do you think that happened? *(forgot to turn the dryer on, dryer's broken, didn't set it to the right temperature, didn't dry long enough)*

4. Amanda poured herself a big glass of milk to drink with her toast. When she tasted it, the milk was sour. Why do you think that happened? *(past expiration date, milk got left out too long before, refrigerator not working right)*

5. José was watching his favorite TV show when it was interrupted for a special news bulletin. Why do you think that happened? *(something important happened that everyone needed to know about)*

6. Whenever Emma pets a dog or a cat, she starts to sneeze and her eyes begin to itch. Why do you think that happens? *(allergic to dogs and cats)*

7. Andrew parked his car and went into the store. When he came back out, he had a parking ticket on his windshield. Why do you think that happened? *(parked in handicapped space, didn't put money in parking meter, parked in illegal parking zone)*

8. Haley was driving home from work. When she got to her street, there was a road block and a sign that said "Road Closed." Why do you think the road was closed? *(road repairs, accident, emergency)*

9. Ms. Carter was flying to San Francisco. She checked her luggage and then boarded the airplane. When she got to San Francisco, she went to the luggage claim area but her bags weren't there. Why do you think that happened? *(bags never got on airplane, airline lost her luggage)*

10. A new movie was showing at the theater. Lots of people went to see it, but many of them left before the movie was over. Why do you think that happened? *(movie was bad, mechanical difficulties with movie)*

11. Faith was working on her computer. She made some changes to a document. Then she turned off her computer and went to bed. When she opened the document the next morning, she discovered that none of the changes she made were there. Why do you think that happened? *(didn't save changes before she turned off computer, something's wrong with the computer)*

12. No one in the country got any mail today. Why do you think that happened? *(It's Sunday, It's a holiday.)*

Inferences 4

Say, "Listen to what I say. Try to picture what is happening in your mind. Then answer the question."

1. The class trip is tomorrow. Only students who have their book reports finished may go. Mary doesn't have her book report done. How does she feel? *(sad, disappointed, mad at herself because she didn't finish her report in time)*

2. Mr. Tinman watched as his son Brandon scored the winning touchdown. How do you think Mr. Tinman felt? *(proud, excited, happy)*

3. The dog is licking the bottom of his empty water bowl. How do you think he feels? *(thirsty)*

4. Richard began to walk faster. There was a strange car following him down the road. How do you think Richard felt? *(frightened, nervous, scared)*

5. Jack woke up this morning with a fever and a headache. How does Jack feel? *(sick)*

6. Maria crossed her fingers. She had spent a lot of time on her painting and really wanted to win the school's art contest. The principal cleared his throat and said, "The winner of this year's art contest is Jamie Hart." How do you think Maria felt? *(sad, disappointed, jealous, mad)*

7. Mrs. Jefferson was up most of the night with her new baby. How do you think Mrs. Jefferson feels today? *(tired)*

8. The neighbor's cat had a litter of kittens. Helen wanted one very badly, but she wasn't sure her grandma would let her have one. When Helen asked her grandma if she could have a kitten, her grandma said, "Yes." How did Helen feel? *(happy, excited)*

9. Izzie's dad is waiting for her. Izzie was supposed to be home by nine o'clock. It's ten o'clock now and she's not home yet. How do you think Izzie's dad feels? *(worried, anxious, angry)*

10. When Martha dropped her tray in the cafeteria, all of the kids laughed at her. How did Martha feel? *(embarrassed)*

11. When Scott came home from school, there was an ambulance at his house. How do you think Scott felt? *(worried, frightened, scared, nervous)*

12. Rachel and her family were camping. Rachel wandered away from the campsite and got lost. How do you think Rachel felt? *(frightened, scared)* When Rachel's mom and dad noticed she was gone, they began to look for her. They found her about an hour later. How do you think Rachel felt when she saw her mom and dad? *(happy, relieved)*

13. Alexa found out her friends went to the mall yesterday without her. How do you think Alexa felt? *(sad, angry, disappointed)* Today Alexa's friends had a surprise party for her. They gave her gifts they had bought at the mall. How do you think Alexa feels now? *(happy, excited, relieved)*

Inferences 5

Say, "Listen to what I say. Try to picture what is happening in your mind. Then answer the question."

1. That sculpture is one of a kind. It certainly is unique! What does *unique* mean? *(one of a kind, nothing else like it)*

2. The fog was so dense we couldn't see the road. What does *dense* mean? *(thick)*

3. I hurried into the room when I heard Zoe shriek. She screamed because she saw a mouse run across the floor. What does *shriek* mean? *(scream)*

4. The earthquake make the ground tremble. People who lived miles away could feel the earth shake. What does *tremble* mean? *(shake)*

5. My parents just purchased a new house. They liked it so much, they bought it right after they looked at it. What does *purchased* mean? *(bought)*

6. I prefer sausage pizza. I like it much better than pepperoni. What does *prefer* mean? *(like better)*

7. This light just won't quit blinking. It's been flashing on and off all day! What does *blinking* mean? *(flashing on and off)*

8. My uncle *resides* in Illinois. He has lived there all his life. What does *resides* mean? *(lives)*

9. The teacher found five spelling errors on my test. I was disappointed because I didn't want to make any mistakes. What does *errors* mean? *(mistakes)*

10. The Sahara Desert is immense. It covers a very large part of Africa. What does *immense* mean? *(very large, huge)*

11. I didn't see the runner slide into home plate. The man in front of me was obstructing my view. What does *obstructing* mean? *(blocking)*

12. Before Sophia accepted her new job, she asked what her annual salary would be. The manager told Sophia she would make about $25,000 a year. What does *annual* mean? *(yearly)*

13. The firefighter made a daring rescue. He saved a family from a burning building. What does *rescue* mean? *(save from danger)*

14. Sometimes Mia can be so stubborn! She always wants to do things her way. She just won't listen to anyone else. What does *stubborn* mean? *(not willing to give in, set on having your own way)*

15. If you put the car in reverse, it will move backward. What does *reverse* mean? *(go backward)*

Inferences 6

Say, "Listen to what I say. Try to picture what is happening in your mind. Then answer the question."

1. We need to leave now. If we linger much longer, we'll miss our plane. What does *linger* mean? *(to stay longer)*

2. The sign said, "Apartment for rent. Inquire within," so I went inside to ask about the apartment. What does *inquire* mean? *(ask in order to learn about something)*

3. Juan was exhausted after football practice. He was so tired he went to bed right after dinner. What does *exhausted* mean? *(very tired)*

4. I get distracted when two people talk to me at the same time. I just can't seem to think clearly. What does *distracted* mean? *(confused, unable to think clearly)*

5. When a skunk is frightened, it lets off a very bad *odor*. I think it's the worst smell in the world! What does *odor* mean? *(smell)*

6. My mom resigned from her job today. She has been talking about quitting for a few weeks. What does *resigned* mean? *(quit)*

7. We have the option of riding the bus or driving our own car. Which would you choose? What does *option* mean? *(choice)*

8. No one could figure out how the thief got into the house. Even the police were baffled. What does *baffled* mean? *(confused, puzzled)*

9. The museum has a large collection of antique dishes. What does *antique* mean? *(very old, made a long time ago)*

10. The movie was so sad it almost made me cry. I was on the verge of tears. What does *verge* mean? *(close to)*

11. After dinner, Grandpa got drowsy. He sat down in his recliner and took a little nap. What does *drowsy* mean? *(sleepy)*

12. I was in my bedroom wrapping a present for my sister, when she knocked on my door. I had to conceal the gift quickly, so I hid it under my bed. What does *conceal* mean? *(hide)*

13. I recently stayed in a hotel near a big airport. I couldn't sleep because the airplanes made too much noise. I had to put my pillow over my head to muffle the sound. What does *muffle* mean? *(make less loud)*

14. Our baseball team is undefeated. Our record is 11 wins and no losses. What does *undefeated* mean? *(not been beaten)*

15. My little brother wrote on my shirt with a permanent marker. I washed my shirt, but the ink wouldn't come out. What does *permanent* mean? *(lasting a very long time, never going away)*

Context Clues

Inferences 7

Say, "Listen to what I say. Try to picture what is happening in your mind. Then answer the question."

1. I'm having a surprise party for my friend. I told everyone I invited, "Mum's the word." What does *mum's the word* mean? *(Don't tell anyone, It's a secret.)*

2. Paige and Jenna are twins. They look alike, dress alike, and even wear their hair the same way. They're just two peas in a pod. What does *two peas in a pod* mean? *(two people who are alike)*

3. Brooke's dad said, "Snap to it, Brooke. We have to leave right away or we'll be late." What does *snap to it* mean? *(hurry up)*

4. Haley can't go to the game tonight. She has a big test tomorrow, so she has to hit the books. What does *hit the books* mean? *(study)*

5. It's late and I'm tired. I think it's time to hit the hay. What does *hit the hay* mean? *(go to bed)*

6. Max told Anna he could hold his breath for ten minutes. Anna laughed and said, "Oh, Max, you're just pulling my leg." What does *pulling my leg* mean? *(joking, kidding around)*

7. Did you see Taylor's new bike? It must have cost an arm and a leg. What does *cost an arm and a leg* mean? *(expensive)*

8. My little brother is always bothering me. He's such a pain in the neck! What does *pain in the neck* mean? *(a bother, annoying)*

9. Emma told David, "The sunset is absolutely beautiful." David said, "You took the words right out of my mouth." What does *take the words right out of my mouth* mean? *(just about to say the same thing)*

10. This report is very confusing. I can't make heads or tails of it. What does *make heads or tails of it* mean? *(understand it)*

11. Julia borrowed her sister's CD player without asking. It broke when she accidentally dropped it. Now Julia has to face the music. What does *face the music* mean? *(take responsibility for her actions, accept punishment)*

12. My friend and I had so much fun at the amusement park. It was a whale of a time! What does *whale of a time* mean? *(great time)*

13. Ashley and Ben went to lunch together. When the bill came, Ben realized he didn't have enough money. Ashley said, "Don't worry about it, Ben. I'll foot the bill this time." What does *foot the bill* mean? *(pay the bill)*

14. Jack was the odd man out. He was the only one not wearing a tie. What does *odd man out* mean? *(different than the rest)*

Inferences 8

Say, "Listen to what I say. Try to picture what is happening in your mind. Then answer the question."

1. I got my report card today and my grades aren't very good. My mom's going to hit the ceiling. What does *hit the ceiling* mean? *(be very angry)*

2. Nicole seems to daydream a lot. She always has her head in the clouds. What does *has her head in the clouds* mean? *(not know what's going on)*

3. Juan is always telling me what to do. I wish he would just get off my back! What *does get off my back* mean? *(leave me alone)*

4. The baby was so tired. When I put him in his crib, he was out like a light. What does *out like a light* mean? *(be sound asleep)*

5. I just started going to a new school. They have so many rules and regulations to remember, it just boggles my mind. What does *boggles my mind* mean? *(confuses me)*

6. We have to try to cheer Tom up. He's been down in the dumps for a long time. What does *down in the dumps* mean? *(sad, unhappy, depressed)*

7. Rachel's dad said, "You can have a party under one condition. Don't go overboard. Keep it simple." What does *go overboard* mean? *(do too much, spend too much money, keep it simple)*

8. My grandpa has a green thumb. He can grow just about anything in his garden. What does *has a green thumb* mean? (can grow plants well)

9. I don't have enough money to buy the TV I want. Will you float me a loan? What does *float me a loan* mean? *(loan me some money)*

10. I don't think I want to listen to Sam sing. He can't carry a tune! What does *can't carry a tune* mean? *(can't sing well)*

11. When I go out with Grace, we never do what I want to do. Grace always calls the shots. What does *call the shots* mean? *(make the decisions)*

12. I hope you get the part in the play. I'm keeping my fingers crossed for you. What does *keeping my fingers crossed* for you mean? *(wishing good luck for you)*

13. Jamie doesn't seem to care that she hurt Keith's feelings. She must have a heart of stone. What does *have a heart of stone* mean? *(be mean or unfriendly)*

14. The meteorologist was completely wrong about the weather. He forecasted a huge winter storm, but we didn't get any snow at all. Now he really has egg on his face. What does *has egg on his face* mean? *(be embarrassed)*

Inferences 9

Say, "Listen to what I say. Try to picture what is happening in your mind. Then answer the question."

1. Clark looks out the cabin window. He sees the Earth far below him.

   Where is Clark? *(spaceship, space shuttle)*
   How do you know? *(can only see Earth if you're in space)*

2. Valerie gets dressed to go outside. She grabs her skis and ski poles as she goes out the door.

   What kind of clothing did Valerie put on? *(warm clothes, coat, gloves, hat, scarf, boots)*
   How do you know? *(It must be cold because she is going skiing.)*

3. Craig is a very strong competitor in the butterfly, front crawl, and backstroke.

   What sport does Craig compete in? *(swimming)*
   How do you know? *(The butterfly, front crawl, and backstroke are all ways to swim.)*

4. Karla took a deep breath and jumped. She fell for about ten seconds before she pulled her rip cord. Then a large cloth device opened up above her like a giant umbrella.

   What is Karla doing? *(parachuting)*
   How do you know? *(She jumped, She pulled a rip cord, A parachute opened above her.)*

5. Laura and her family are going to St. Louis, MO. That's where they'll join the wagon train. After her dad hitches the horses to the covered wagon, Laura climbs into the back.

   When is this story taking place? *(pioneer days)*
   How do you know? *(That's when people traveled in wagon trains.)*

6. Adam thought the four faces carved into the side of the mountain were awesome. He knew each of their names: George Washington, Thomas Jefferson, Theodore Roosevelt, and Abraham Lincoln.

   Where is Adam? *(Mt. Rushmore, South Dakota)*
   How do you know? *(It's the only place in the world where the faces of four Presidents are carved into a mountainside.)*

7. The man put on his armor, grabbed a weapon and a shield, and walked into the arena. When they saw him, thousands of people began to cheer. The man entertained the crowd by fighting a lion.

   Who is this man? *(gladiator)*
   How do you know? *(fights in an arena, wears armor and carries a weapon, entertains a large crowd)*

Extending Conversations

Students often have a difficult time maintaining an appropriate, meaningful conversation. The dynamics of a conversation are amazingly complex, encompassing listening and verbal skills as well as myriad nonverbal factors, including facial expressions, hand gestures, and physical proximity.

This brief section contains some guidance for your students in approaching the art of conversation, as well as opportunities to practice specific conversational techniques. As your students work through these pages, monitor their abilities in these areas (model appropriate behaviors as needed):

Verbal Factors:
- tone of voice appropriate for audience
- speaking pace is neither too fast nor slow
- speaks clearly and loudly

Listening Factors:
- paraphrases information
- asks appropriate questions
- waits turn to speak (doesn't interrupt)

Nonverbal Factors:
- maintains interested eye contact (not staring)
- proper body proximity
- proper posture

The above factors are, of course, a very basic list of skills needed in a successful interaction. Encourage your students to practice these good habits as they work to build more meaningful conversational skills.

Extending Conversations 1

Photocopy this page and give copies of the bottom half to your students.

Say, "You probably talk to all kinds of people every day. You talk to your friends, your teachers, and your family. There is often a difference between "talking to" people and having a "conversation." A conversation is a way of talking that allows two people to share information and get to know one another better. This section will help you learn some skills to have better conversations. This diagram shows you the basic things you need to remember to have a good conversation."

- -

Here are some things to keep in mind during your conversation.

Eye Contact	Keep eye contact with the person. Don't keep looking away. Pay attention by keeping your eyes on your partner.
Posture	Sitting up or standing up straight lets your partner know you're interested and ready to talk and listen.
Wait	Wait for your turn to speak. Don't interrupt.
Distance	Stay a comfortable distance from your partner. Don't "crowd" or "drift away" during your conversation.
Speak Clearly	Speak clearly. Don't mumble, talk too quickly, or too quietly. Use a confident, calm tone of voice.
Listen Carefully	A conversation is only successful if you both listen. Pay attention to what your partner says. Be ready to ask a question or say something about the topic.

Extending Conversations 2

Say, "The best way to take part in a conversation is to have something to say. A good place to start is to answer a simple question. Answer each of these questions with at least three good reasons or responses. Use complete sentences to answer. Here's an example:

> What makes someone a good teacher? *(A good teacher is someone who knows a lot about different subjects. Good teachers also listen and answer questions. A good teacher cares about all students.)*"

(Note: Answers will vary.)

1. What is your favorite time of day and why?

2. What are some things you like about going to school?

3. What are some things you don't like about going to school?

4. Who is your favorite band/singer and why?

5. What are your favorite outdoor activities?

6. What are your favorite indoor activities?

7. What is a great way to spend a Saturday morning?

8. Describe what you think is perfect weather.

9. Describe what you think is rotten weather.

10. Tell me about your favorite dinner.

11. What are your least favorite foods and why?

12. What is your favorite place to be and why?

13. What is your favorite game or sport to play and why?

14. What is your favorite TV show or movie and why?

15. What are some things that you're really good at doing?

Extending Conversations 3

Say, "The best conversations require a lot of listening and asking questions. If you listen carefully to what the person is saying, you can ask questions to get more information. I'm going to read you part of a conversation and some questions you might ask to learn more from the speaker.

'Last week we went to the beach with my aunt and uncle and our cousins. We packed a cooler full of food and had a great time. We were there for the whole afternoon. I ended up getting a bad sunburn but it was still fun.'

Some questions you might ask to learn more are:

What beach did you go to?	How many cousins do you have?
What are your cousins' names?	How old are your cousins?
What did you have for lunch?	What things did you do all afternoon?
Were you wearing sunscreen?	Does your sunburn still hurt?

Now listen to each of these bits of conversation. Ask as many questions as you can think of about what was said."

(Note: Answers will vary. Some sample questions have been provided.)

1. You won't believe what happened last night! My dad came in the door with a brand new puppy. The puppy is so cute but he cried all night long. This morning Dad looked a little tired and not too happy about our new family member. *(Where did your dad get the puppy?, What does the puppy look like?, What kind of puppy is it?, Why did the puppy cry?, Why was your dad tired?)*

2. I'm glad my mom is feeling better. She was sick for two days and didn't get out of bed. I had to take care of my little brother the whole time. That was not much fun, and I couldn't leave the house. I think Mom was glad I could help out. *(What was wrong with your mom?, Did she go to the doctor?, Why did you have to take care of your brother?, Why couldn't you leave the house?)*

3. There was a huge storm at our house last night. We saw a bunch of lightning and then BAM! There was a giant explosion and all our lights went out. Mom went outside to have a look but didn't see anything because it was so dark on our street. It was a pretty cool sound, though. *(What happened?, Did lightning hit something?, Was your mom scared to go outside?, How long were your lights out?)*

4. I played this cool video game over at Brian's place yesterday. You get to be this giant robot trying to save a city from the enemies. It was hard but Brian's big brother helped me learn how to play. His brother is so good at video games and he's a nice guy too. *(What was the name of the video game?, Why was it hard?, What is Brian's brother's name?, Why is he so good at video games?, Where does Brian live?, Did you win the game?)*

5. I caught the first fish of my life last weekend. I didn't even know what I was doing. Luckily Grandpa was there because the fish was huge. I thought for sure that fish was going to break my pole. It was bending over so far it almost touched the water. But Grandpa helped me pull the fish into the boat. *(How much did the fish weigh?, Where did you go fishing?, What kind of fish did you catch?, Did you have fun?, Did your grandpa catch any fish?, What was the boat like?)*

Extending Conversations 4

Say, "One way to keep a conversation going is to paraphrase what your partner says. When you paraphrase, you say something in your own words about what the person is talking about. This might seem silly, but it's important to a conversation. It lets the person know you've been listening carefully. After you paraphrase, follow up with a question to keep the person talking. Here's how it works:

Speaker:	My mom is learning to use a computer for work. She's having a pretty tough time. Every night she reads a different computer book. I hope she gets it figured out soon. She's been in a bad mood for over a week now!
Your Paraphrase:	It sounds like your mom is having a tough time learning to use a computer.
Your Question:	What have you been doing to try to help your mom?

Listen to what each speaker says. Then paraphrase what's been said and ask a question that will keep the conversation going."

(Note: Answers will vary. Some sample questions have been provided.)

1. I usually love playing Monopoly, but not with my cousin. He came over last night and wanted to play so I said, "Yes." But after a few minutes I noticed he was taking extra money and putting it on his pile. I told him I saw him cheating, but he said I was lying. I know I saw him cheat. *(I don't think I'd want to play with someone who cheats. What will you do if he asks you to play a game with him again?)*

2. My mom let me help get dinner ready last night. I've never really wanted to learn to cook but it was a lot of fun. She did all the cooking on the stove, and I helped make the salad and do some other stuff. There's a lot about cooking I never knew. We had a good time. *(It sounds like you found a new hobby. What are you going to try to cook next time?)*

3. I'm glad Mr. Kelso is back this week. We had a substitute teacher for three days, and she wasn't sure what to do. She seemed nice, but we were supposed to be finishing our project on the planets. The substitute told us we'd have to wait until Mr. Kelso got back to finish. Instead we just had to do a bunch of boring worksheets. *(You'd probably be finished with your project by now if Mr. Kelso hadn't been gone. Do you think you'll finish it this week?)*

4. We went on a field trip to a recycling plant last week. It was amazing. They showed us how they take plastic containers and turn them into stuff that can be used again. First they chop up all the containers. Then they wash them and melt them down. When the plastic cools, they chop it up again and sell it to people who make new plastic things. *(That sounds like an interesting field trip. I always wondered what they did at a recycling plant. What other field trips have you taken this year?)*

5. Corey fell asleep on the bus last night and forgot to get off at his stop. When he woke up he realized that he was way past his stop. He didn't get scared though. He just laughed a little and went right back to sleep. He's a strange guy sometimes. *(I never would have been able to go back to sleep if I knew I'd missed my stop! How did he get home?)*

Extending Conversations 5

Say, "Keeping a conversation going isn't all that hard if you know how to do it. You have to remember that each person in a conversation is responsible for making it work. Many conversations follow a similar pattern of people giving information and asking questions. In this exchange, one person asks a question. Then the next person answers the question and asks a question back.

> Speaker 1: I get so nervous before a test. Even if I've studied and I know my stuff, I'm still scared that I'm not going to do well. How do you feel before a test?

> Speaker 2: I don't really get nervous. I usually feel like I know what most of the questions will be like. Why do you think you get so nervous?

Listen carefully and answer each question that you're asked. Then ask another question of the speaker to keep the conversation going. Make sure you stay on the same topic, and try not to answer a question that can be answered with one word. That's a sure way to kill a conversation."

(Note: Answers will vary. Some sample responses have been provided.)

1. Some people think that someday there won't be any books. They say everything we need to know will be on computers. I'm not so sure about that. What do you think will happen to books in the future? *(I don't know. I can't imagine a world without books, but I guess it could happen. Lots of people read books for entertainment. What would those people do?)*

2. My teacher says I have really sloppy handwriting. She says she can't read my writing. When I take my time I can make it look neat, but I hate spending that much time writing. Besides, if I take all that time I probably won't get my assignments done on time. What do you think I should do about this problem? *(I wouldn't want to get bad grades just because my teacher couldn't read my writing. I think I'd try to write neater or maybe type my assignments on the computer. Did you ask your teacher if you could type your assignments?)*

3. There was a huge fire in our neighborhood last night. I think there were at least ten fire trucks there. It was incredible to see all those people working to put out the fire. Even with all that work, the place still burned almost to the ground. Have you ever seen a big building fire like that? *(No, and I hope I never do. Was anyone hurt?)*

4. I don't have any proof, but I think my parents are looking through my room when I'm gone. Sometimes when I get home I notice stuff moved that I hadn't touched. I know they won't let me lock my door, and there's nothing in there I'm trying to hide. What do you think I should say to them about this? *(I think I'd just ask them if they've been in your room. What do you think they're looking for?)*

5. My big sister decided to become a vegetarian. She said she's not going to eat any more meat. She might have fish once in a while but that's it. I really don't care what she does, but now she keeps bugging me about eating meat and saying I should be a vegetarian too. How do you feel about people who eat meat? *(I think people should be able to eat whatever they want. If your sister doesn't want to eat meat anymore, that's fine, but I don't think she should be bugging you about it. What are you going to say to her?)*

Nonverbal Communication

Observing and interpreting a speaker's nonverbal communication is as important as hearing and interpreting what the speaker says.

> Is the speaker shouting? Why?
> What does the speaker's facial expression indicate?
> What does the speaker's posture suggest?
> What do the speaker's gestures and eye contact tell you?

Even though few students receive direct instruction in nonverbal communication, most students have picked up a great deal of knowledge about nonverbal communication by the time they enter third grade. They know the difference between a sincere and an insincere "I'm sorry." They know when the teacher is mildly irritated vs. annoyed vs. downright angry. They know when someone is telling them something in confidence and when someone is being sarcastic. Most students, though, can't verbalize how they know these things because they have little or no experience thinking or talking about specific nonverbal cues and their impact on communication. More importantly, some students don't even recognize nonverbal cues. Since about 90% of understanding a speaker depends on nonverbal factors, we must teach nonverbal language as part of "good listening."

Students who don't understand and use appropriate nonverbal communication are at risk for misunderstanding others and being misunderstood themselves. Here are some of the ineffective nonverbal behaviors that can alienate students from their peers:

- fidgeting

- using poor eye contact (e.g., avoiding eye contact, not including all group members, not signaling turn-taking appropriately, etc.)

- giving nonverbal signals that interrupt others

- pausing too long before responding to others, especially without giving a reason for the delay

- using an inappropriate speaking voice (e.g., monotone, inappropriate pitch, inappropriate volume, hypo/hypernasality, etc.)

- standing too close or too far away from others

- touching (or pushing) others inappropriately

- making unnecessary body noises (e.g., throat clearing, sniffing, snorting, burping, etc.)

- using inappropriate facial expression (e.g., lack of expression, excessive expression, mismatch between feelings and intended expression)

- using inappropriate posture (not matching their mood or attitude)

- offending others by lack of cleanliness or grooming

Nonverbal Communication, *continued*

Talking about discrete aspects of nonverbal communication helps all students boost their listening skills, especially for the meaning and emotions behind a speaker's words. Practicing nonverbal communication skills helps students evaluate their own communication styles and refine the ways they communicate with others.

Here are some general guidelines for teaching your students about "listening" to nonverbal language:

- Talk about paying attention to nonverbal cues as an important part of "good listening."

- Exaggerate whatever nonverbal cues you're highlighting for your students. Explain what each nonverbal message is saying.

- Point out how nonverbal cues can reinforce your words, contradict your words, or substitute for words.

- Draw attention to a specific nonverbal cue you give your students during the day, such as raising your eyebrows, shrugging your shoulders, or raising your voice.

- When you observe good nonverbal cues from a student, explain what you noticed and how it helped you understand what the student was communicating.

Begin teaching your students about whole-body cues first. Work toward more discrete nonverbal cues as your students are ready to incorporate them into their listening.

Recognize that as your students get older, there will probably be increasing differences between boys and girls in some aspects of their nonverbal communication. For example, girls may be comfortable being very close to each other during conversation, while boys may prefer to avoid body contact with each other.

Basic Information

Explain the difference between verbal and nonverbal communication.

> Verbal communication means what people say.
> Nonverbal communication means how people talk, whether they use words or not.

Have a brief discussion about nonverbal communication to prepare students for the activities ahead. Tell them that good listeners pay close attention to nonverbal communication; up to 90% of what we "hear" is based on the speaker's nonverbal messages, not the words the speaker says. Here are some examples of nonverbal communication to demonstrate and talk about with your students:

Facial Expression
- smiling vs. frowning
- raised eyebrows
- lips pressed together tightly (tension or firm resolve)
- open mouth with a slack jaw
- winking
- sneering

Body Posture and Gestures
- waving hello/goodbye
- slumping
- erect posture
- guarded/protective (making body as small as possible)
- shrugging your shoulders
- pointing

Voice
- using a loud voice vs. a soft voice or a whisper
- using a high-pitched voice vs. a low-pitched voice
- using an expressive voice vs. a monotone voice
- speaking with a scratchy voice vs. a smooth, clear voice
- humming
- whistling
- sighing
- yawning
- clearing your throat to get attention

Space and Touch

- standing very close vs. somewhat apart from someone
- shoving or nudging someone
- patting someone on the back
- touching someone to get attention

Rhythm and Time

- talking very quickly or very slowly
- taking a long time to respond to another speaker
- interrupting someone
- being on time vs. being late

Hygiene and Grooming

- dressing neatly vs. sloppily/haphazardly
- having combed hair vs. uncombed/unkempt hair
- eating with your mouth open vs. closed
- having offensive body odors

"Listen" to My Face

Demonstrate a variety of facial expressions and ask your students to guess what you're "saying" with your face. Reinforce all logical guesses and talk about what specific parts of your face you used to get the message across. Talk about how your eyebrows, eyelids, gaze, nose, and mouth are or aren't involved in specific expressions. You could also include the angle of your head or your upper body postures.

Eyebrows communicate significantly in American culture, so help your students notice what eyebrows add to messages. Use the same facial expression twice, but cover your eyebrows for one demonstration. What do your students notice?

Give your students a copy of the picture on this page as a visual cue while you talk about the three zones of facial expressions.

Zone 1 — forehead and eyes

Zone 2 — nose and cheeks

Zone 3 — mouth

Nonverbal Communication, *continued*

Use an index card to cover each zone of your face while you make common facial expressions. Ask your students to judge which zone gives the most important information. Help them discover that Zone 2 conveys much less information than Zone 1 or Zone 3; covering your eyes deletes key information for portraying emotions or emphasis.

Next distribute mirrors to your students. Ask them to watch themselves making faces in a mirror. What can they say with their eyes? What about with their mouths?

Then have your students practice being mirrors themselves. Have them reflect, or copy, someone else's facial expressions as though they are mirrors.

Group the students into pairs of boys or girls. One partner will be the mirror, reflecting the other person's exact facial expressions. Encourage the non-mirror students to change their facial expressions slowly to give their "mirrors" a chance to change with them. Some students may have difficulty noticing the specifics of someone's facial expressions well enough to imitate them so point out specifics to help them, such as:

> "Notice how he's raising one eyebrow more than the other one."

> "She's opening her eyes really wide. See how you can see her whole eyeball?"

> "Notice how he's pressing his lips together tightly."

After a few minutes, have the partners change roles and repeat the activity. Afterward, talk with your students about what they noticed during this activity.

If your students are embarrassed to do this activity with each other, give them magazine pictures of people's faces with varying expressions, and have your students mimic one picture at a time while they look in a mirror to check their imitation. Begin with faces with exaggerated expressions and progress to more subtle expressions. Encourage your students to talk about what they notice to increase their fluency in observing and commenting on nonverbal cues in facial expressions.

Cartoons often use eyebrow, eye, and/or mouth cues to enhance characters' messages. Bring in some cartoons and talk with your students about how various cartoons use facial expressions to enhance characters' messages. Then encourage your students to draw cartoons and include appropriate eye/eyebrow lines to depict characters' emotions.

Posture Cues

Explain that posture is the position of your body. You can "listen" to someone's posture to guess the person's feelings or attitude about something. If possible, show a videotape of people without the

Nonverbal Communication, continued

sound, preferably featuring a variety of emotional reactions to situations. Stop the tape frequently to ask your students what someone's posture is "saying." If you can't play a videotape, use pictures of people in various postures.

Demonstrate body postures to signal some of the feelings listed on page 166. Use a chair and other props as appropriate to get your posture message across. Exaggerate your postures at first, but as your students pick up speed guessing your body messages, adopt more realistic/less exaggerated poses. Try to keep your facial expression neutral in the beginning, but eventually adopt facial expressions that also reflect your general message.

Once your students grasp this concept, do the activity on page 165. Copy the page and cut the stimuli apart. Give one stimuli to a student and have the student assume an appropriate posture to convey the message or feeling. The other students can guess what the student is portraying.

If students guess an appropriate message for a student's posturing, tell them they are correct. Then use this opportunity to explain that the same posture can often mean more than one thing. Ask, "What else could (student) be saying with this posture?"

Also caution your students that people's postures don't always reflect their true feelings. For instance, you can slouch (fatigue, boredom), yet be perfectly happy. Tell students they are more likely to be understood if their posture shows how they really feel.

Nonverbal Communication, continued

Posture Cues Activity

Use these stimuli with the directions on page 164.

I look exceptionally cool today!
I'm jealous of you.
This is the most boring class in the world.
I'm really sorry.
That's disgusting!
I have something really exciting to say!
Don't bother me. I'm angry!
That music hurts my ears.
I'm sick to my stomach.
I'd love to know what's going on over there!
I'm really worried.
I'm nervous.
I'm thrilled!

Walking Messages

The way someone walks gives a signal about the way the person feels. Your students will have fun "listening" to distinctive ways of walking that "talk." Designate a walking space about 12 feet long. Have volunteers take turns demonstrating a walk that shows a specific feeling. Whisper the emotion to each walker and give the student time to think of an appropriate walking style. Then have other students guess what the walker was "saying" via the walking style. Here are some emotions to try:

- embarrassed
- mildly afraid
- terrified
- proud
- surprised
- shy
- nervous
- jealous
- curious
- confident

- thoughtful or pensive
- assertive
- mopey
- enthusiastic
- miserable
- guilty
- tired
- vain
- defeated
- rushed

Help your students notice what specific nonverbal cues convey the intended emotion.

Gestures

Give your students a few examples of common gestures like the ones listed below. List these so everyone can see. Then work with your students to expand the list. Demonstrate each gesture and have your students echo your demonstration. Explain that most gestures involve the hands, fingers, shoulders, and/or arms.

Common Gestures	Meaning
wave	Hi or goodbye
finger to lips, lips out	Shhh!
finger to lips, lips closed	Hmm, I wonder . . .
thumb up	Way to go!
thumb down	No way!
shoulder shrug	I don't know. I don't care.
hands on hips	I'm angry.
hand extended, palm up	Give it to me.
hand extended, vertically	Let's shake hands.

Common Gestures, *cont.*	**Meaning,** *cont.*
first finger up, fist	I've got it! Here's an idea!
high five	Congratulations! Good job!
raised arm, hand up	I know the answer.
pointing to self	I, me
arm out, hand straight up	Stop!

If possible, show a videotape and pause to comment on people's gestures. You could also play charades to demonstrate the communication power of gestures.

Personal Space

Explain that personal space is like a bubble of air around you. You want the air bubble bigger between you and a stranger than between you and a friend.

Draw (or tape) a circle about one yard in diameter and stand in the middle of it. That's an average bubble or space Americans are comfortable surrounding themselves with as an "intimate zone." We like this amount of space between us and a friend or someone in our family when we're talking about personal things or feelings.

Draw (or tape) another circle surrounding the intimate zone, this one four feet from the center. This is the personal zone we use for most conversations.

Next draw (or tape) a circle 12 feet in front of the center of the intimate zone. The area between 4-12 feet is our social zone. In this zone, you may need to raise your voice volume, and you should not talk about personal or private information as it is a public zone.

Finally explain that the public zone is anything beyond 12 feet. It is too far away for normal conversation, so we usually use facial expressions and/or gestures to communicate with people.

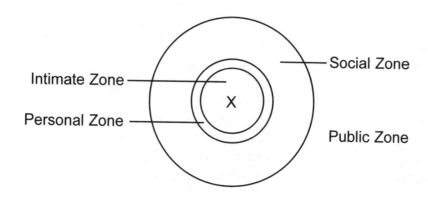

Nonverbal Communication, *continued*

Although this framework is generally comfortable for most Americans, people differ in their personal comfort with space. The key for your students is to learn to "listen" to the different space requirements different people need in order to feel comfortable. Here are some signals you have been a space invader:

- The person backs away from you.
- The person turns away from you.
- The person avoids looking at you.
- The person won't talk to you.
- The person frowns at you.
- The person gets angry at you.

There are times we need to be space invaders. Then we need to warn the person by saying "excuse me" politely before we invade. Here are some situations in which we need to be polite space invaders:

- Your pencil rolls under someone's desk and you want to retrieve it.
- You need to pass in front of people in a row of seats to get to your seat.
- You need to go through a line to keep heading where you're going.
- You need to reach in front of someone in a cafeteria line.

Help your students imagine personal air bubbles around other students to remember not to invade their space. When they need to invade, help them remember to excuse themselves politely.

Some students also violate space expectations in these ways:

- Talking too loudly in a personal or an intimate zone
- Talking too softly from a distance
- Talking about personal things from a social zone

Copy *Keep Your Distance*, page 169, and cut the strips apart. Draw (or tape) a ten-foot line at the front of the class. Have a student stand at one end of the line. Then have the other students take turns reading a strip and standing an appropriate distance from the stationary student.

Nonverbal Communication, *continued*

Keep Your Distance

Use these stimuli with the directions on page 168.

You are a best friend. You want to tell a secret.

You are a teacher. You want to compliment the student privately.

You are a stranger. You want to know how to get to the school office.

You are a waiter. You want to take the person's order.

You are the person's brother. You want to show a cut finger.

You are a parent. You want the person to come to dinner.

You are a nurse. You want to check the person's blood pressure.

You are a new student. You want to know the person's name.

You are the person's friend. You want to know why the person is sad.

You are the person's parent. You want to have a private conversation.

You are a stranger. In a movie theater, you are in line behind the person.

The person's leg is hurt. You are a classmate. You want to help the person walk to the nurse.

You are a stranger. The person is sitting on a park bench. Sit on the same bench.

The person is playing a video game. You are a stranger. You want to play the game next.

You don't get along with the person. The teacher wants you to tell the person it's time to come inside.

Voice Cues

If possible, audiotape a variety of voices saying a brief message. Record people your students probably wouldn't recognize by voice alone. Play one voice at a time and ask your students, "What do you notice about this person's voice?" Guide your students to make inferences about the person's age, emotion, gender, etc., to emphasize that people's voices give us impressions that might or might not have anything to do with the words they're saying.

Some of your students might enjoy imitating voices of famous cartoon or movie characters. Talk about how these voices suit the characters or people.

Intonation

Demonstrate how much we can "hear" from a person's tone of voice by saying the same message with different intonations. Here are some example messages for this activity:

- Great, it's time to get up and get ready for school.
- I love to hear your sister practice her piano.
- I can't wait to get our tests back.
- You're a great friend.
- That's the end of the line back there.
- That's not what you told me yesterday.
- No one asked me to be on a team.
- I can't wait to see what Leo is wearing.

Try to suggest these kinds of intonation patterns:

- whining, feeling sorry for yourself
- curious, as though you're amazed how this happens
- angry, as though you blame someone or something
- whispered, as though you're sharing a secret
- congested with a bad cold
- self-centered, as though you're immature
- enthusiastic
- worried

Nonverbal Communication, continued

Word Emphasis

This activity highlights the way we emphasize specific words to change the whole meaning of the actual words we say. Students who fail to grasp the significance of this kind of word emphasis are at risk for misunderstanding what they hear.

Write "I want to leave now" where students can see it. Tell your students you're going to say that sentence several times. Ask them to think about whether you mean the same thing each time you say the sentence. Then say the sentence four times, emphasizing a different word each time. Depending on your delivery, this sentence might mean the following:

I want to leave now. (Whether anyone else wants to leave now or now, I definitely do.)

I **want** to leave now. (It's my own choice to leave now.)

I want to **leave** now. (I don't want to do anything but leave.)

I want to leave **now**. (I want to leave right this second.)

Guide your students to detect the differences in meaning and to tell how they knew the differences. For visual reinforcement, underline a word in the sentence and demonstrate emphasizing that word.

Page 172 lists additional sentences that could have very different meanings, depending on the words emphasized when the sentences are spoken. Put page 172 on an overhead or copy it and distribute it to your students as a handout. Have students take turns saying each sentence as many ways as they can to communicate different messages or feelings that go with the actual words.

Nonverbal Communication, *continued*

Use these sentences with the directions on page 171.

Say, "Say each sentence as many different ways as you can."

1. You make me so happy.

2. I apologize.

3. You copied my homework answers.

4. This isn't about you.

5. You can't come with us.

6. I think I could do it.

7. I was sitting there.

8. What do you want to know?

9. I'll help you later.

10. You're always late.

11. What's up?

12. I've never talked to her.

13. This game is easy to win.

14. You know all my secrets.

15. Whose smelly socks are these?

16. What's your address?

17. The next one is my favorite.

18. You seem really nervous.

Rhythm

Good listeners recognize the rhythms speakers use and know what they mean. We use rhythm to express emotions and attitudes. We are generally more comfortable interacting with someone using the same rhythm as ours. A mismatch in rhythm can turn off a conversation partner. For example, if Speaker A is using a slow rhythm while talking about a personal problem, Speaker B could seem uninterested by responding with a rapid pace. Likewise, if Speaker A talks rapidly to show enthusiasm, Speaker B could seem uninterested by responding lethargically.

The first step is to become aware of different speaking rhythms. If possible, play audiotapes of people speaking at different rates and ask your students to talk about each speaker's rhythm. What does it suggest about the speaker? For example, a fast speaker may project enthusiasm, tension, or discomfort, and a slow speaker may project boredom, ignorance, or depression. Some speakers use the same speaking rate for almost all conversations, while others vary their rate depending on their emotion or the purpose for the conversation. Also, some cultures speak more rapidly or more slowly than others. For example, Southerners often talk more slowly than New Yorkers. Help your students to consider emotional as well as cultural factors in evaluating various speaking rhythms.

To highlight the importance of matching rhythms, ask a pair of students to walk across the room together. They will probably walk with similar rhythms. Then ask one student to walk more slowly than the other. Do they still seem to be walking "together"? Do they seem as interested in each other as when they walked at the same rate together? Use this visual exercise to show how it feels when your conversation partner uses a different speaking rate.

Use the role-playing situations of *Matching Rhythms*, page 174, to help your students practice matching their speaking rhythm to someone else's. Let the first speaker set the pace for the conversation; the second speaker should listen carefully and match the first speaker's rate in responding. Have other students evaluate each role-playing pair.

Nonverbal Communication, continued

Matching Rhythms

Cut these role-playing situations apart and give one to a speaker in each conversation pair. The speaker should use the situation and dialogue (in italics) to begin a conversation with the suggested speaking rate.

Your math test has been cancelled. Speak rapidly to show your excitement.
"Wow, did you hear the news? Our math test was cancelled!"

Your dog is very sick. Speak slowly to show your concern.
"Our dog is really sick. We had to leave her at the vet's."

You are in a hurry because class is about to start. Speak quickly.
"I can't find my house key. No one will be home when I get there today."

You see a strange dog running toward you. Speak quickly.
"Watch out, there's a dog coming right behind you!"

You are giving someone directions. Speak slowly.
"First look in the cabinet for some paper cups. Put them on the table."

You're apologizing. Speak slowly.
"I'm sorry I took your pencil without asking you first."

You're disappointed in your report card. Speak slowly.
"I didn't do very well this time. I didn't turn in all my homework."

You fell off a scooter and your arm really hurts. Speak quickly.
"I think I might have broken my arm! It really hurts!"

You're sleepy because you stayed up late. Speak slowly.
"I can't remember what we're supposed to do for homework."

You're hurt because a friend didn't ask you to her party. Speak slowly.
"Why didn't Kenya invite me to her party? She's my best friend."

19-08-98765